"A moment with Jesus will set you fr[...] Jesus will keep you free. Noah Herrin [...] in the church with a timely message that I truly believe needs to be heard. I would highly recommend *Holy Habits* to anyone who is looking to grow in intimacy with Jesus Christ."

Jentezen Franklin, senior pastor, Free Chapel;
New York Times bestselling author

"In a world of shallow, the next generation needs a voice of their own that's pointing them to the deep. In *Holy Habits*, Noah Herrin provides this generation with some practices they can spend a lifetime developing and deepening."

Carey Nieuwhof, founder, The Art of Leadership
Academy; bestselling author, *Didn't See It Coming*

"In this amazing book, Noah Herrin gives ten practical habits that will make a giant positive impact on your life. Noah shows us how these changes are easy to implement but make a powerful impact! This book is a helpful read for anyone wanting more from Christianity."

Jonathan Pokluda, lead pastor, Harris Creek Baptist
Church; podcast host, *Becoming Something*;
bestselling author, *Welcome to Adulting*

"*Holy Habits* will help you run the race of life. Noah is committed to the long game of following Jesus faithfully, and he's created a practical and timely guidebook for putting the habits in place not only to run the race but to finish the race well."

Brad Lomenick, former president, Catalyst; author,
H3 Leadership and *The Catalyst Leader*

"Transformational truth for every age. Our everyday decisions determine our intimacy with God. Noah challenges the reader not simply to read but also to practice the presence of God. Daily surrender creates a miraculous life of legacy. You will be so encouraged with every chapter. The impact of what he shares will last long after you finish reading!"

Rich Wilkerson Jr., pastor, VOUS Church, Miami, Florida

HOLY
HABITS

HOLY HABITS

10 Small Decisions

That Lead to a Big Life

Noah Herrin

Chosen

a division of Baker Publishing Group
Minneapolis, Minnesota

© 2023 by Herrin Ministries, Inc.

Published by Chosen Books
Minneapolis, Minnesota
www.chosenbooks.com

Chosen Books is a division of
Baker Publishing Group, Grand Rapids, Michigan

Printed in the United States of America

ISBN 978-0-8007-6340-4 (trade paper)
ISBN 978-1-4934-4227-0 (ebook)
ISBN 978-0-8007-6359-6 (casebound)

Library of Congress Cataloging-in-Publication Control Number: 2023019799

Personal stories of individuals in this book are used by permission. Some identifying details of certain individuals have been changed to protect their privacy.

The author is represented by the literary agency of A Drop of Ink LLC, www.adrop ofink.pub

Baker Publishing Group publications use paper produced from sustainable forestry practices and post-consumer waste whenever possible.

23 24 25 26 27 28 29   7 6 5 4 3 2 1

To Lion,
the one who made me
the luckiest dad in the world.

CONTENTS

FOREWORD

In our world of instant everything, we can be prone to opt out of the spiritual disciplines God wants to use to shape our lives and build our futures. If we are not careful, we end up exchanging the on-fire life of faith God has for us with anemic spirituality bound to personal comfort. No wonder so many Christians experience so much less than what God wants for them. It's time to go back to the basics, and that's why *Holy Habits* is a book the church needs right now!

I am thankful not only that Noah wrote this book, but that he approaches this topic with both humor and candor. Between stories of his love for queso and his fear of Home Depot, Noah provides practical ways to reignite passion for God and sustain that passion in day-to-day life. There's nothing more essential as Christians than cultivating a deep relationship with God, and these pages will encourage you in your walk with Jesus and help you go to new depths in the life of faith.

Now, before you begin reading, here is something you need to know about the author. Noah is the real deal. He and his wife, Maddy, are living out what you are about to read. This content has been road tested in their lives. They are passionate followers of Christ and have a conviction that God wants you to experience the life-changing power these habits can produce in your relationship with Jesus. This book is a firsthand example of Noah and Maddy's heart to see people strengthened and encouraged in their faith journey.

As you dive into *Holy Habits*, make reading each chapter a holy moment. Lean into what God wants to do in your life. Expect that the Holy Spirit is going to personally apply these pages to your life. Anticipate that as you put these habits into practice, you will watch God lead you to a new place in your walk with Him.

John Lindell, senior pastor, James River Church,
Springfield, Missouri

INTRODUCTION

I spend a lot of time inside of churches. Last year I preached a total of eighty-eight times. I find myself at Christian conferences more often than most people find themselves at the gas station. Because of my job (calling, passion, or whatever you'd like to call what I do for a living), I feel like I have a pretty good idea of what is going on in the American Christian world. In almost every setting I find myself, no matter the age or background, the idea of growing in intimacy with Jesus is always something that is talked about. Intimacy with Jesus is a huge part of the Church's vocabulary, but is it a part of our daily schedule?

We've got loads of talented Christians, that much is certain. I'd argue there has never been a time in earth's history where there have been more talented followers of Jesus than right now. We've got the most incredible worship leaders, teachers, pastors, songwriters, media directors, and vocational ministers that I've ever seen inside the Church. But we've also got the most amazing actors, doctors, nurses, teachers, songwriters, authors, military members, dentists, marketers, construction workers, athletes, trainers, engineers, and marketplace workers who love Jesus, too. Our talent is extraordinary. Our work is consistently getting better. But what about our relationship with Jesus? Is that going "up and to the right" on the chart as well?

Richard Foster, one of my favorite authors ever, once said, "The desperate need today is not for a greater number of intelligent people, or gifted people, but for *deep* people"[1] (emphasis added). Even though Foster penned those words over forty years ago, they are just as true now as they were then. Talented people are everywhere. Deep people are truly rare.

A deep person is someone who has roots, which has very little to do with talents, abilities, or even intellect. Depth is created in people by what they repeatedly do and who they believe they are. Specifically, depth is created in a follower of Jesus when he or she moves beyond the surface into the depths of a relationship with God. It is created when people regularly put themselves in a position for God to speak to them, refine them, and build them back up.

When life gets hard, our work for Jesus does not keep us close to Him, the depth of our relationship with Him does. When a worldwide pandemic hits, our intelligence does very little to keep our faith levels high, but our intimacy with Jesus certainly will. When everything else is stripped away from the surface of our lives, the deepest parts of us will emerge. Are you deep? Would you describe your relationship with Jesus as *intimate*?

I love Sunday morning church services. You might think I'd get tired of church services with how often I participate in them, but that is not the case. If anything, my love for them grows. There is nothing like worshipping God next to friends and family in the context of the local church. Serving God's people while being in the presence of God with the intention of growing together is special.

I love conferences and events, too. There is something unique about the expectancy that we, as believers, have for conferences. We show up believing that something life-changing is going to happen, and often it does. I've had many mountaintop moments with God at Christian conferences. I've had experiences at conferences where I've repented of sin, made purposeful commitments to God, and even been set free from sinful addictions. The reality of church services and conferences is that while they can absolutely mark our lives forever, they are not the foundation of real intimacy with Jesus.

Real depth, the kind that followers of Christ should be hungry for, is only attained in the context of a personal relationship. In any relationship, intimacy grows best in a one-on-one environment. If I want to grow closer to my wife, I can do that by going to a baseball game with a few of our closest friends. We can grow closer by attending a concert together and making memories with 30,000 others, dancing and singing. But our relationship will grow exponentially deeper by having intentional, daily conversation in the privacy of our front porch. The *best* way to cultivate intimacy is through the habit of pursuing it, one-on-one.

It works the same way with Jesus. Intimacy with Jesus grows in the context of our daily habits with Him. Our habits shape our days, our days shape our seasons, our seasons shape our years, and our years shape our lives. And, when all is said and done, our lives shape our eternities.

An ungodly life begins with ungodly actions. Ungodly actions quickly become ungodly habits. Likewise, a holy life is built on intentional, holy habits. Paul writes about this very thing:

> Whoever sows to please their flesh, from the flesh will reap destruction; whoever sows to please the Spirit, from the Spirit will reap eternal life. Let us not become weary in doing good, for at the proper time we will reap a harvest if we do not give up.
>
> Galatians 6:8–9

Paul is saying that your actions matter. Your habits matter. This truth is also taught outside of Scripture. James Clear, who is widely recognized in the secular world as the official expert on habits, says this: "Every action you take is a vote for the type of person you wish to become."[2] Our habits are forming the future us.

What kinds of votes are you casting for tomorrow's version of you? Are they leading you to become the person you want to be? Are those decisions helping you growing holier? Deeper in your walk with Jesus? Is your life going to be one that you are proud of?

It's been said, "Show me your friends, and I'll show you your future self." The implication is that your friends have a massive impact on your life. They definitely do. I would just argue that your habits have an even greater impact. Show me what you repeatedly do, and I'll show you who you'll eventually be.

Sowing and reaping is a massive biblical theme. Where you sow will reveal where you will grow. If you repeatedly sow habits of the flesh, you will continually grow in your desires of the flesh. If you repeatedly sow habits of the Spirit, you will continually be growing in the image of Christ. Where are you sowing?

It is important to note, however, that the power of spiritual habits is not found in the habits themselves. Reading your Bible by itself does not draw you closer to God. There are many atheists who spend time in Scripture. It's when the holy habit is combined with the presence of the holy God inside of us that our habits truly become transformative. A holy habit plus the presence of a holy God equals life transformation. We have to be intentional, and not do things just to do them, but rather *so that* we might see God.

When my wife, Maddy, and I first got married, she did what any good wife would do: She helped me decorate our house and turn it from an ugly bachelor pad into a beautiful home. One of the things she was set on was adding plants throughout the house. Even though I'm allergic to every green growing thing on the planet, I agreed to this because of how beautiful it made our home. "It was a vibe," as the kids say.

A few weeks after we added a particularly pleasant-looking plant to our living room, the plant started to go from lush green to light brown. I remember my wife complaining in her sweet southern accent that she didn't know what was happening to it. She was watering it regularly, trimming the excess branches to make room for new growth, she was even encouraging it each morning with her words. Yet it still wasn't growing.

Eventually, she solved the mystery: The plant was positioned too far from the window. It was getting some indirect sunlight throughout the day, but not near enough to allow it to flourish. Once Maddy moved the plant in front of our main living room window, it thrived.

Our daily habits are the act of getting our souls in front of the one true, living God. The power is not in the habit itself, but something transformative happens when we regularly place ourselves in front of Him, expecting Him to show up. Our daily habits put us in the right environment that leads to our flourishing in Christ. The most Jesus-like people I have ever met are not the most famous or well-known. They are those who have simply built habits that put them in front of Jesus on a daily basis, and have stuck with those habits for years. Consistency leads to intimacy.

Growth in our relationship with Jesus is stunted when we don't regularly spend time with Him. We can also regularly do things *for* God without doing things *with* God, which equally stunts our growth in intimacy with Jesus. The goal of this book is to help you build holy habits that will increase your intimacy with God, which will result in His powerful transformation of your life.

Massive spiritual results always start with small, daily decisions. Conferences can take us high; our habits take us deep. Church services on a Sunday morning can include great fellowship; our habits are a great foundation. An encounter with Jesus will set us free; our spiritual habits will keep us free. An encounter with Jesus introduces us to Him; our daily habits allow us to get to know Him.

Before you read *Holy Habits*

For a long time, my dad was an avid scuba diver. He loved being in the water. He would regularly hop on a boat with friends, sail out to the middle of the Gulf of Mexico, and dive down to the ocean floor to take in the beauty of God's creation. He would come back with photos of all sorts of incredible creatures. He has pictures of whales, sharks, an octopus, and even a selfie with a sea turtle.

I've learned a lot about scuba diving through the experiences of my dad. I've learned more effective ways to swim and fight the pull of the tide. I've learned that dolphins love to travel in little communities called pods. I've learned that if you get seasick and throw up your lunch, you quickly become the fish's best friend as they swarm for an all-you-can-eat buffet.

Perhaps the most interesting and important lesson that I've learned about scuba diving is the "art of the descent." If you had never been scuba diving for yourself (or don't have a dad who did it regularly), you might think that if you want to take in the beauty of the ocean floor, you just dive down to the bottom and look at it. That's definitely what I thought: The quicker you can get down there, the better. This couldn't be further from the truth.

Any experienced scuba diver will stress the importance of going deep slowly. When you descend too deep too quickly, the barometric pressure of the ocean can do funny things to your body. In some cases, those funny things can quickly turn deadly. Divers must allow their bodies to get acclimated to the new environment before proceeding to the deep. Reaching the beautiful sights in the depths of the ocean is a journey that must be taken intentionally and slowly.

My prayer for you as you read *Holy Habits* is that by implementing these habits into your everyday life, you will find that there is so much more to a relationship with God than an hour service on a Sunday or the occasional devotional you might read. My prayer is that you would trade a snorkel out for scuba gear and submerge in the boundless riches of God's grace to the depths of intimacy with the Lord.

But before you keep reading, there is something you need to know: Going deep is a process that is often slower than we expect. We live in a culture and world that has made instant gratification possible in nearly every area of life. We are obsessed with speed. We want things, and we want them now! The reality is that most of the time you can get whatever you want rather quickly. But that's not how a deep relationship with God works.

I've watched it countless times in the life of a Christian. They have a life-changing encounter with God and are immediately filled with an unquenchable passion to know God intimately. So they start reading their Bible, going to church, and buying every Christian Living book they can find on the Amazon bestseller list. They are excited, and they are ready to dive to the ocean floor of knowing God. Then something tragic happens. A few weeks or maybe months pass, and they slowly, maybe even unconsciously, lose their zeal. They didn't try to. But when the results didn't match their passion, they swam back up to the surface. Just as the slow descent in diving is important, the intentional, consistent effort of going deeper with God is pivotal.

God operates on a different kind of timeline. He is stubborn with His timing, and rightfully so. After all, He knows best. He knows what we need and when we need it. He does not desire souls who swim to the bottom, take the photo for Instagram, and swim immediately back to the top. He wants our relationship with Him to get better and better, from now until eternity. He wants us to desire the bottom of His heart, but He also wants us to enjoy the journey of getting there.

If we want to go deep with God, we must adjust our expectations. The goal of this journey is not to see results; the goal of this journey is to see God and to enjoy Him. That's what He desires from us.

As you read this book and implement the habits discussed in its pages, I encourage you to go slowly. If you don't constantly practice any of the ten habits, it would be foolish to try to implement all of them at once. Add one, then observe yourself for a few weeks. Learn when the best time is for you to practice it. Take careful notes on what things cause you to miss the habit, or help you keep it. Have conversations with friends about what you are doing. Give yourself time for the habit to stick before adding another one.

Another wise thing to know is that the results will likely look very different from one habit to the next. You may implement a habit like "Rest so you can run" and immediately feel closer to God and hear from Him in ways you've never heard from Him before. But you might implement "Read it and choose it" and not see real results for a long time. That's okay—keep at it! Remember, we are looking for God, not results.

It is much healthier to look at these habits as a long-term investment account that compounds exponentially over time, rather than looking at them as a get-rich-quick scheme. God's grace and our salvation through the finished work of Jesus is the closest thing we have to a get-rich-quick scheme. We are saved immediately, praise Jesus! But real intimacy takes time. Real growth takes digging, planting, watering, and waiting.

So don't give up on a habit when you don't see immediate results. Keep fighting to be consistent. Keep fighting to see the Lord. Keep fighting to go deeper.

A holy habit works best when it has actually become a habit. Habits, and intimacy, take time.

Read It and Choose It

I LOVE QUESO DIP. *Love* it. On the eighth day of creation, I'm pretty sure God spoke queso dip onto our dinner tables. Hallelujah. One of my favorite questions in the world is: "Would you like to start your meal by ordering some chips and queso?"

Why yes. Yes I would.

When I go to a Mexican restaurant, it's not even a question. We are getting a large bowl of the queso. We are going to be "dipping and chipping." Salsa is a good thing, but queso dip is a God thing! C'mon somebody!

Here's some free advice for you on the first page of this book: Stop letting people treat you like the free salsa. You are the *cheese dip*! I digress.

I obviously love queso cheese dip. But queso does not always love me back. Does that make sense? Sometimes it gives me a stomachache. I am, at a minimum, lactose intolerant. At maximum, I am queso explosive.

The first date I ever went on with my now-wife, Maddy, was a group date at a Mexican restaurant. I was on my best behavior. Not only was I sitting across from my literal dream girl, but three of her closest friends had also joined us on the trial run. I didn't just have one person to win over, I had four.

Our waitress greeted the table and got our drink order. Then, just as she was about to leave, she asked the great question, "Would you guys like some queso as an appetizer?"

Immediately a battle waged in my mind. On the one hand, I *always* ordered the queso. No matter what it did to my stomach, the cheese was always worth it. On the other hand, I couldn't afford to mess this up. What if the cheese dip decided to ruin my life? What if I got knocked out in the first round of dating by an appetizer?

Before a victor could be crowned in the battle in my mind, a decision was made for me: "We'll take two of them!" one of Maddy's friends said.

Checkmate.

I'd love to tell you that when the cheese dip got to our table, I displayed an extreme amount of self-control and that I didn't touch it. I'd love to report to you that I am in fact stronger than my cravings. But that would be a falsehood. The sad reality is that the moment I laid eyes on our appetizer, I began to lie to myself.

Your stomach isn't that weak anymore—you've grown, Noah. You're strong now.

You shouldn't be afraid of lactose. Lactose should be afraid of you.

God hasn't given you a spirit of needing to use the bathroom, but one of power, love, and a sound stomach.

I ate the queso. And it was good, so I ate a lot of it. It took all of ten minutes for my stomach to start "arguing" with me. This wasn't a hushed tones kind of an argument either. My stomach was singing Taylor Swift break-up songs to me in the middle of that restaurant. "Weee are never ever ever . . . getting back together!"

One of Maddy's friends could tell something was wrong and asked if I was okay. I don't know if it was the noises my stomach was making or the one lonely tear slowly rolling from my left eyeball that gave me away. To this day, I legitimately do not think I have ever had a stomachache like that in my life.

Okay—enough about stomachaches. Enough about queso. Enough about lactose. Please don't stop reading this book because I shared my dairy issues with you in the first chapter. The real problem of my story isn't any of those things. The real problem is in the lie that I told myself. I knew I shouldn't have eaten the cheese dip. I knew it wouldn't end well for me (especially on a first date with my dream girl). And yet there was a little voice inside my head that did not tell the truth. And I listened to it.

In today's world, people have extremely different opinions on pretty much everything. It's hard to get large groups of people to agree about even the simplest of subjects. One of the few remaining shared beliefs of our day is that lying is bad. No one wants to be told a lie. That doesn't end well. No one wants to be known as a liar, either. But perhaps even worse than either one of those is when someone *lives* a lie. Living a lie has led to the destruction of countless individuals, families, and entire communities. Living and believing lies holds free people captive.

Throughout the course of this book I'm going to use the term *freedom* quite a bit. It's important for me to explain up front what I do not mean by that word. What I do not mean is your freedom of rights. I'm not talking about your freedom of speech or right to bear arms. I'm not alluding to the freedom that comes from getting out of credit card debt or choosing your favorite football team to root for. All of those freedoms are worth writing about. But this book is focused on another kind of freedom.

I'm talking about a freedom found in the Bible. A freedom that Jesus promised, David prayed for, and Paul wrote about. I'm talking about the freedom from sin, addiction, and fleshly desires that plague us all as human beings. The freedom that is granted to us when we decided to put our hope in Jesus Christ as Lord and Savior. That freedom is real.

But that freedom is *always* under attack. The greatest threat to you as a follower of Jesus in today's climate and culture is not Jeff Bezos or Mark Zuckerberg. It's not Russia, China, or some other country. It's not a social media app. It's not even a virus, vaccine, or doctor. The greatest threat to your freedom as a follower of Jesus is a small, four-letter word: L-I-E-S.

Whether you realize it or not right now, you are in an all-out battle for your freedom in the arena of truth versus lies. This is not a new battle for human beings. It has been this way from the beginning when Satan went to war with Eve. Do you remember his weapon of choice? A lie. Satan deployed lies to steal freedom then, and he does the exact same thing today.

Jesus called the devil the father of lies. "When [the devil] lies, he speaks his native language, for he is a liar and the father of lies" (John 8:44). His effectiveness is not just in the amount of lies that he tells, but in the cleverness of his lies.

Today he even disguises his lies with cute little cultural phrases like "Be true to yourself." That one always gets me laughing. My response is usually, "Which self?" I've got a lot of me's! One day I think Crocs are a horrible choice for shoes, the next day I'm buying two pairs. One week I might avoid gluten, the next week I'm not even sure I know what gluten is. Sometimes I'm a gym junkie like Troy Bolton, getting my head in the game, other times I skip the gym for Chick-fil-A. There are shifting levels of self.

The devil is not just lying to our culture but to Christians, too. And there is one lie that is absolutely wreaking havoc on believers all over the world today. It's the lie that *God's priority is to make us happy.*

"Wait, Noah—that's a lie? God doesn't want me to be happy?" It's not that God doesn't want you happy. It's just not His priority. But the devil loves telling you that it *is* God's priority. Satan would love for you to make life decisions believing that happiness is God's true goal for your life. If he can get you to do that, you will make choices based on the best interest of your feelings instead of the best interest of your faith.

You may feel like leaving your marriage one day because it doesn't *feel as good* anymore. Because God just wants you happy, your marriage must not be from God.[1] You might leave the church that you used to love because it doesn't *feel exciting* anymore, instead of being faithful to where you were planted. You'll be tempted to remove yourself from rich friendships the moment one of your friends cares enough to call you out or hold you accountable about something. Instead of seeing them as a friend who cares about your walk with God, you'll feel like a victim and cut someone who loves you out of your life.

Do you see how buying into the lie that God just wants you to be happy can actually ruin your life? Following Jesus has a cost—it just so happens that not following Him costs a lot more.

God's priority for our lives is not to make us happy. It's to make us holy. This is why God sent Jesus in the first place. God wanted to have a relationship with us more than anything else in the world. However, the only way to have a relationship with a holy God is to be holy ourselves—which just so happens to be impossible for sinners like us. So God in heaven, in His infinite mercy and grace, sent His only Son, Jesus, down to earth to die for all of our sins. Not so that we would be happy, but holy. So that we could live in communion with God for the rest of eternity. It just so happens that our holiness eventually leads to our happiness when we realize how great Jesus is.

Holiness is not, however, a destination that we "arrive" at. It looks a lot more like a fight. Holiness is hard. Holiness is a daily invitation to come and die. It's the same invitation Jesus gave to the earliest disciples in all four gospels. Do you remember Jesus' words? "Whoever wants to be my disciple must deny themselves and take up their cross daily and follow me" (Luke 9:23).

The cross wasn't just something for Jesus; it's for us, too. Holiness is a fight, because many times the last thing we want to do is pick up a cross and walk to our death. The death of our pride, selfishness, preferences, feelings, habits, addictions, lust, greed, and all the rest of our flesh. Holiness is a journey where we follow Jesus, and as we do, we progressively get better and better at saying no to our flesh and yes to the ways and thoughts of Jesus. Holiness is simply choosing truth over lies.

Not long ago, I started working out at a CrossFit gym. If you're wondering what that has to do with this book, let me explain that when you sign up to start CrossFit, part of the agreement is that you will tell everyone you know that you now do CrossFit. I tease. People who do CrossFit workouts tend to be pretty passionate and talk about it a lot.

It started when my wife and I were expecting our son, Lion, to be born; I got out of shape. I was on the road traveling and speaking a lot, and I let my diet and workout habits slip. I could see the "dad bod" coming on faster than I had anticipated. I started trying to do little at-home workouts, but they just didn't seem to be working. I remember thinking that fat cells must know Jesus as their

Lord and Savior because those things seemed to have eternal life. So I went to a CrossFit gym to see what all the fuss was all about. Maybe they could help me.

During my first visit, I was a mixture of amazed and terrified. The people inside were legitimately the most fit people I had ever seen in my life. But they were also doing some of the weirdest and most intense exercises I had ever seen. Upon seeing me, the gym owner Alec (now an awesome friend) came over and introduced himself to me. I told him about my predicament and asked if he could show me around and explain the concept more.

For the next twenty minutes, Alec pitched me on why CrossFit was "perfect" for me. You know what Alec conveniently left out of the conversation? How my body was going to hurt. He didn't tell me that there would be many mornings when I would come home and just lie on my living room floor like roadkill. He never once told me how early the classes were in the morning. He didn't even tell me about the diet changes I'd have to make. He left all of that important information out of our conversation.

Alec spent our entire time together talking about how awesome CrossFit is. He told me how much better I would be able to move because of it. He introduced me to some guys who looked like Greek gods and alluded to how I too could be Hercules. He talked about how much better I would feel each day and how it would probably lead to a longer life. He spent all of our time talking about the *benefits* of doing CrossFit.

Alec understood a principle that also applies to us spiritually: that a life driven by negatives rarely leads to a positive. Another way to put it is that if your focus is on what you can't do, you'll never be thankful for what you *get* to do.

Holiness has a cost. Choosing truth over lies is not easy. It hurts. Some days you might feel like roadkill lying in your living room floor. But holiness also has benefits. And if our desire is to be people who fight for holiness on a daily basis, we have to remind ourselves why it's so worth it.

What are some benefits of holiness, you ask?

- an increasingly intimate relationship with the Creator of the universe
- the future joy of a fifty-year marriage anniversary
- peace that surpasses all understanding
- a family that loves each other and stays together (even if Thanksgiving might be a rollercoaster)
- the fulfillment that comes from living your life for the sake of others
- purpose—having a calling from God
- the hope of eternal life
- community that helps carry your burdens

If I were to list all of the benefits of holiness, it would take up the rest of this book. These are just a few of the rich benefits of choosing truth over lies. A holy life is not just about saying no to our flesh, it's about saying yes to true life.

31

Even God's no is for our good. When we buy into the vision and the plan that God has for our lives, we are simultaneously signing up to see our lives thrive in the best way possible. God's way.

Without the pursuit of holiness, you'll never have the intimate relationship with Jesus you desire. Sin is an intimacy killer. Grace is an intimacy saver. Holiness is an intimacy grower. When you begin to live a holy life, your desire to have holy habits will only grow. And as you put holy habits in place in your life, you will grow in holiness.

So how do we do this? What's the *play* that we run in order to live holy lives? Remember the Scripture in John that I referenced earlier in the chapter? Don't worry, I've got it for you again: "Then you will know the truth, and the truth will set you free" (John 8:32).

I love this verse deeply, but it can be extremely misleading. You can read these words from Jesus out of context and think, *All I have to do is know the truth to be set free.* What about the people who know Jesus as Lord but still haven't been set free? What about those who have accepted Jesus into their hearts but are still addicted to pornography or worship their bank accounts? What about the people who have heard the truth of the Bible but still tend to "live my own truth"?

Chances are, if you've been following Jesus for a while now, you've heard John 8:32 quoted hundreds of times. But I doubt you've heard the verse before it nearly as often. Check this out:

To the Jews who had believed him, Jesus said, "If you hold to my teaching, you are really my disciples. Then you will know the truth, and the truth will set you free."

John 8:31–32

Let's back up and provide a little context. The first thirty verses of John 8 are fascinating. Jesus is talking to a very large crowd of people. He tells them that He is the Son of God (can you imagine your neighbor telling you that at the grocery store?), He calls out some sin in the people's lives, and He even alludes to the fact that He is one day going to die for all of them! Those are pretty outrageous claims, and to many they came across as absolutely crazy.

By the time we get to verse 31, the crowd had gotten much smaller. Notice the verse starts off with "To the Jews who had believed him"—the only people left to hear the words that would come next were the people who decided to believe. If you believe Jesus, you should listen up to what comes next; it's for you too: "If you hold to my teaching, you are really my disciples. Then you will know the truth, and the truth will set you free."

This is life-changing—stay with me. These people *already* believe in Jesus, they have heard the truth, they even believe the truth. And yet, that alone is actually not enough to set them free. What does Jesus say? "If you hold to my teaching . . . then you will know the truth, and the truth will set you free." That first part is what often gets left out. It starts with *knowing* the truth, but it has to lead to choosing the truth in order to live a holy life.

This is why reading the Bible daily is so important. You'll never choose the truth if you don't know it. And if you never choose it, then you'll never live it. You might *know* the truth, but you won't live free.

Remember when we talked about how holiness is a fight? This is the battle. When the devil lies to you and tells you that you will always be your old self and that your identity is tied up in your old ways, first of all, be encouraged, because bringing up your past means he's running out of new material. Then, remember: You fight the lie with the truth. "Therefore if anyone is in Christ, the new creation has come: The old has gone, the new is here!" (2 Corinthians 5:17).

And when the devil lies and says you are a victim, you fight with the truth: "But thanks be to God! He gives us the victory through our Lord Jesus Christ" (1 Corinthians 15:57).

When the devil lies and says that you are not important, you fight with the truth: "For you are a people holy to the LORD your God. The LORD your God has chosen you out of all the peoples on the face of the earth to be his people, his treasured possession" (Deuteronomy 7:6).

When the devil lies and says that you can't be hurting and also be close to God, you fight with the truth: "The LORD is close to the brokenhearted and saves those who are crushed in spirit" (Psalm 34:18).

This is why reading the Bible daily is so important. You'll never choose the truth if you don't know it. And if you never choose it, then you'll never live it. You might *know* the truth, but you won't live free.

When the devil lies and says you should be afraid, you fight with the truth: "The LORD is my light and my salvation—whom shall I fear?" (Psalm 27:1).

When the devil lies and says that no one even notices you, you fight with the truth: "You are the God who sees me" (Genesis 16:13).

When the devil lies and says that the storm is too great to bear, you fight with the truth: "We have this hope as an anchor for the soul, firm and secure" (Hebrews 6:19).

Why do we know the Word of God? It's not for the sake of knowledge alone. It's so that we can choose to live the truth instead of the lie. It's for the sake of the battle!

Fighting for your peace is worth it.

Fighting for your faithfulness is worth it.

Fighting for your joy is worth it.

Fighting for your purity is worth it.

Fighting for your marriage is worth it.

Fighting for your kids is worth it.

Fighting for your friends is worth it.

Fighting for your legacy is worth it.

Fighting for your holiness is worth it.

Maybe you're reading this and thinking that this all sounds a bit daunting. The Bible is big, and you aren't much of a reader. Maybe you just have a hard time understanding what you're reading when you open it. Or maybe you've never opened it at all. All of that is okay.

I'm about to give you an easy habit. It's simply a repeatable action. Over time, this action will be something you go from consciously making time for to something you crave. It will help set you free from the lies that enslave you. After this habit becomes part of your normal routine, I believe you will look up one day and realize that the temptations that used to cause you to sin no longer even tempt you.

HABIT: READ IT AND CHOOSE IT

Where it comes from: Matthew 4:1–11 and John 8:31–32

What it is: Fighting the devil's lies and temptations, by reading the truth *and* choosing the truth, so we can live holy lives unto the Lord.

How to run the play: What are the lies the devil tells you the most? What are the temptations you face daily? Full transparency: For me, the devil really attacks me with lies about money. That we won't have enough to make ends meet, that I'm not doing a good enough job providing for my family, etc. That lie could easily lead to me not trusting God. It could lead to stress that I take out on my family. It could lead to money being an idol in my life. There are other lies he tells me on a regular basis, but this is one of the main ones he comes after me with. It's important to recognize those lies.

Go buy a small notebook. Or grab a piece of paper or something else to write on—just don't lose it, and make sure it's small enough to keep with you. On the top of the page, identify the lie. Then, expose it by writing the truth. For example, mine looks something like this:

> Lie: You should be stressed out about money. It's up to you to provide more for your growing family, and if you don't, you are a failure because it's completely up to you.

> Truth: "Look at the birds of the air; they do not sow or reap or store away in barns, and yet your heavenly Father feeds them. Are you not much more valuable than they?" (Matthew 6:26).

The play is that simple. You think about and ask God to help you identify the lies the devil throws at you regularly. Then, you turn to God's truth to replace the lie. If you aren't sure what Scripture verse fights the lie told to you, there are some things you can do.

1. A quick Google search will get you on the right start. "What are some Bible verses about____?"
2. Ask your local pastor or a mentor. Find someone who has been following Jesus a little longer than you and ask them if any Scriptures come to mind that will help you fight that particular lie. Chances are they will know several.

Fill your notebook with as many lie-and-truth combos as you need. I currently have about sixteen in mine. (I am continually searching my heart and mind, reading and choosing the truth.) Whenever your mind comes under attack, pull your notebook out and declare the truth.

Maybe that looks like reading the verse out loud once or twice. Maybe that looks like reading it and silently praying for God to give you the strength to choose the truth and for the lie to no longer have control of your mind. You will discover what is most comfortable for you.

Over time, not only will the lie lose its power, but you will get so used to the truth that fights the lie, you might not even need to open the notebook. The truth of Scripture will already be in your mind and heart. That's the goal. That's how you win the fight.

Read it and choose it.

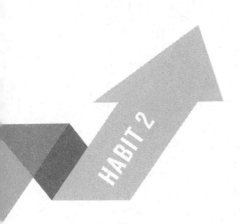

Get Good at Coming Home

WHEN I WAS IN THE FIFTH GRADE, I crashed my bike into our neighbor's mailbox.

It was bad. I didn't have a "fender bender" with the mailbox; I totaled it. I hit that mailbox so hard that I sent it straight to its grave, priority mail. Where there was once a beautifully painted white, wooden mailbox, now stood a small stump protruding from the ground.

I remember panicking immediately. I looked around the neighborhood to see if anyone had witnessed the home-owner's association crime that had just been committed. I felt embarrassment. Then I felt fear of what my dad was going to say when he found out. Then I felt a burning sensation on my knee and looked down at my injury. The situation wasn't great.

I spent the next hour riding around our neighborhood on my bike trying to figure out what to do. I knew for sure I was going to be grounded. That much was certain. I was just trying to figure out how to minimize my punishment as much as possible. I pedaled through the streets of Plant City, Florida, feeling awful for my neighbors, awful for myself, and awful for my parents.

Finally, I went home. I walked into the kitchen. "Dad . . . I hit the Patels' mailbox with my bicycle." Don't get me wrong, my dad was not stoked to hear that news. But his reaction surprised my eleven-year-old self. He asked me if I was okay. He gave me a big hug. He walked outside to assess the situation. He rang the doorbell and apologized to the neighbors for me. He paid for the mailbox to be fixed (there was a greater chance of that mailbox fixing itself than me or my dad doing it—we are horrible with tools). We went and got root beer floats to cheer up. The rest of the day actually went well.

I think when we mess up spiritually, often our first reaction is not what it should be. We feel the shame. We feel the embarrassment. We feel the weight of our failure and we sit in it. We try to scheme our way out of the feelings. We spend some time driving around the neighborhood, trying to figure out the best way to handle the situation. We put ourselves in a spiritual time-out. We do everything but the only thing that can truly solve the problem: come home. One of the most dangerous lies we could believe as followers of Jesus is that we have to wait to come home.

When we sin, come up short, or make an embarrassing mistake, the temptation is to go anywhere but home. The temptation is to take a lap and try to figure it out. The lie is to believe that there is a way to fix the situation without the help of our Dad.

We see a similar story in the Bible. In Luke 15, a son runs off with his inheritance. He makes mistake after mistake and blows everything he received from his father. He finally makes his way back home, and the father's reaction is shocking.

> While he was still a long way off, his father saw him and was filled with compassion for him; he ran to his son, threw his arms around him and kissed him.
>
> Luke 15:20

The father saw the son coming while he was *a long way off*. This implies that the father had been eagerly looking for the son, awaiting his return. Did you know when you turn your back on God, He never turns His back on you? Did you know that God would rather have a struggling son than no son at all? A struggling daughter than no daughter at all? Did you know that while you are trying to figure out how you could possibly approach Jesus with your mistakes, He is eagerly waiting for you to just come home?

To me, the craziest verse in the Bible is Hebrews 12:2: "For the joy set before him he endured the cross . . . " What was pushing Jesus on to endure the pain and suffering of the cross? What possible joy could offset the nails driven through his hands and feet? How could someone be suffocating on His own blood yet be filled with purpose?

When we sin, come up short, or make an embarrassing mistake, the temptation is to go anywhere but home. The temptation is to take a lap and try to figure it out. The lie is to believe that there is a way to fix the situation without the help of our Dad.

He was looking ahead to the moment that you would come home.

Jesus knew there would be no way for you to know Him intimately if He didn't endure the cross. He knew you didn't have the power to fix the mailbox on your own. He knew you couldn't possibly pay for your sin by yourself—so He did it for you. He endured the cross, His eye on the joy, because He is a far greater lover than you are a sinner. He is a far better chaser than you are a runner. He is way better at being good than you are at being bad. He is a far better Savior than I am a son.

Chances are that you already understand this idea. This is not a new thought to a follower of Jesus, it is simply the Gospel. That He who knew no sin became sin so that we might become right with God (see 2 Corinthians 5:21). We come home and accept the sacrifice Jesus so generously poured out for us on the cross. We come home to be saved.

When I say "come home," what I mean, of course, is to come back to God. We were all made in his image (see Genesis 1:27). God originally walked with Adam in the Garden of Eden (see Genesis 3:8). Man was once home with Him, but after Adam's sin, our sin nature caused a break in that relationship.

The moment you accepted Christ into your life, you came home. You had your own Luke 15 experience of realizing that your heavenly Father was running to you with arms wide open. My question for you, the believer, is a simple one: Do you still come home?

I haven't met a single sinner who accepted Jesus and then stopped sinning. Does life change for new believers?

Absolutely. Does the way they talk change? Yes. Do their habits change? Most of the time. But we are weak, and the devil is sneaky. Sin rears its ugly head in the life of even the closest Jesus follower.

When sin shows back up in your life, what is your response? Does it cause you to go on a binge of reckless living, like the son in Luke 15? Where sin compounds exponentially before you return home? Does it cause you to be filled with shame and condemnation as you take a lap around the neighborhood and try to figure out what to do? Do you put yourself in a spiritual time-out and try to hide from God, like Adam and Eve did in the Garden? What do you do? What should you do?

You should come home. Believers come home to be saved, but many resist coming home to be changed. True transformation can only happen through the presence of Jesus. Shame has no power to change a heart, but Jesus does. Time away from God won't fix the problem. Time with God will.

Proverbs 24:16 says, "Though the righteous fall seven times, they rise again." It does not say that the unrighteous may fall, but the righteous. The difference between the unrighteous and the righteous is not that one falls and the other does not. The difference is that one falls and stays down while the other gets back up. The righteous come home.

Another important observation in this verse is the number used to describe how many times the righteous fall: seven. The number seven is often used throughout the Bible to signify something that happens numerously, or to signify infinity. So when we see the number seven in this verse, we know that the righteous fall *a lot*. I used to think, *Well, if I fall more than seven times, I must be toast.* This is not the case! The reality is that we, as the righteous, all fall a lot. We just get up a lot, too.

We get good at coming home. Home is where we are forgiven. Home is where we are restored. Home is where our heart is changed. Home is where our sinful desires are replaces with God's holy desires. Home is where we must go as quickly as we possibly can.

The habit we are really talking about in this chapter is repentance. My favorite definition of repentance is to turn *away* from something, and then turn *toward* something else. If you are reading this as a follower of Jesus, chances are you said a prayer of repentance the day you accepted Jesus as your Lord and Savior. You decided to turn away from your sin and turn toward Jesus and His grace for you. Repentance is a beautiful thing.

In the last few years, so many Christians have asked me to share my thoughts on repentance. Almost all Christians believe repentance is required at the time of salvation. That part is not debatable. But there is a large theological controversy surrounding the question of whether repentance is necessary once you've already been saved. In other words, people want to know if they have to keep repenting every time they sin.

Some believe the answer to that question is yes. Some believe it is no, that the grace of God covers all past, present, and future sins. Both camps can be pretty passionate about their convictions. To me, asking whether it is necessary is the wrong question. The question should be, Is repentance helpful?

My answer to that question is an overwhelming *yes*. When I repent, I am choosing to turn from my sin, my shortcomings, my flesh, my selfishness, and turn to Jesus. I am making an active decision to draw near to God in those moments. And I know from Scripture that when I draw near to God, He always draws near to me.

The habit of coming home is the habit of turning from *and* turning to. We turn to Jesus, believing that the more we look at Him, the less we will want to look at what we are so easily tempted to look at. It's the habit of repenting our way into greater intimacy with Jesus.

When I was in college, I battled an addiction to pornography. This was a battle unlike any other I'd faced, and it lasted for years. Even before I was following Jesus, I knew that the porn was crushing me. Day by day I grew more anxious, depressed, tired, and I was beginning to lose focus in every area of my life. Porn is a killer.

When I accepted Jesus as Lord and Savior of my life, I just assumed the struggle with porn would stop. I thought that the presence of Jesus in my life would mean the disappearance of my sinful nature. Boy was I wrong.

The next few months of my life were exhausting ones. The days when I didn't look at porn, I felt close to God. If I didn't look at porn for an entire week, I felt *really* close to God. But there were many days I stumbled. Those days I felt far from God. The shame, anxiety, and condemnation I felt on those days were sometimes unbearable. I knew what I was doing was wrong, and I still was doing it. I knew Jesus died for me willingly, and my response was to keep going back to the thing that was killing me!

It wasn't like I wasn't trying to stop. I read books on quitting. I listened to sermons about lust. I even had an accountability partner. Nothing seemed to work. I look back on those tired, sad, and frustrating days now with thankfulness. As of the morning that I am writing this chapter, I am almost six years free of pornography.

What eventually broke that cycle of sin in my life was simple. I fell more in love with looking at Jesus than looking at porn. I came home enough times to realize that what was at home with Jesus was so much better than what I was finding through my flesh. I was saved from my sin by Jesus Christ, absolutely. But I was set free from my addiction by the habit of repentance.

I've met with dozens of young men who have shared the same struggle. They have all described the same feelings of deep shame and have wanted to know what worked for me. What did I read? What advice did I receive? I tell them to go home. The moment I stopped waiting to repent was the moment I started taking ground in my battle.

Before, I would look at the porn and be filled with regret and immediately feel like there was no way I could spend time with Jesus for a while. I would often skip church because of it. I would take a few days off from praying or reading my Bible. I felt like I couldn't come home.

But then one day something happened. I had just looked at porn and was struggling with the same usual emotions of that moment when I felt the sudden urge to repent immediately. Would God accept such a quick repentance?

Would He see that as me taking advantage of His grace? I didn't know. But I was desperate. I remember my prayer to this day because it would become something I would pray regularly for several months: *God, I am so sorry. I know what I just did is not who I am. Please forgive me. You are so much better than I deserve. Thank You for knowing about this part of me and still sending Your Son to die for me. I love You.*

I don't know how many times I prayed that prayer, but it was a lot. Probably more than fifty different times I prayed those words right after looking at porn. The day came when I had the urge to sin the way I had been sinning for years, but I didn't. My desire was to look at porn, but my desire to be with Jesus was just stronger. I remember pressing into my newfound confidence in who I was.

Now my repeated prayer has become, *God, I am tempted right now, but I am no longer defined by my feelings or emotions. I am not a slave to them—I am a slave to You. Thank You for Your grace that has covered me so many times and led me to a place where I can say no.*

It wasn't that porn stopped being attractive to me. It was simply that Jesus started becoming more attractive. I had turned away from porn and straight to Jesus so many times that my heart had begun to change. Old desires were replaced with new desires. Old thoughts were replaced with new thoughts. I was becoming what Paul refers to in the New Testament as a "new creation" (2 Corinthians 5:17). My relationship with Jesus was growing intimate by the habit of repentance.

The takeaway from this chapter is a simple one: Get good at coming home. It's easy to mistake the heart of our heavenly Father: He doesn't just love you, He *likes* you. Jesus' reaction to sinners is one of compassion and gentleness. How can you possibly come back home so soon? Because Jesus is the most approachable person of all time. He is crazy about you. He wants you to approach Him with your sin. It is literally why He came to die—so that He could take the burden of sin off you and place it on Himself.

HABIT: GET GOOD AT COMING HOME

If there's a specific sin that you can't seem to shake, begin the habit of immediate repentance. It will feel weird at first. A feeling of *Should this be allowed?* will come in the beginning. But continue to follow these simple steps for coming home:

1. Ask for forgiveness of the sin.
2. Accept His grace: Jesus forgives you.
3. Focus on the *goodness* of Jesus.

Your prayer can be as long or as short as you'd like. Follow the prompting of your heavenly Father. Talk to Him like you know Him, because you do.

As you grow in the habit of coming home and habitual sin has less and less of a hold on you, a great place to add this habit is in the morning. I've found that I think clearest after a cup of coffee. During that time each morning, I practice a short habit of repentance that follows these steps:

1. Invite God to search my heart.
2. Ask for forgiveness.
3. Accept the grace of Jesus by receiving His forgiveness.
4. Request a new heart.

This prayer normally doesn't take me long. But many mornings, as I've asked God to search my heart, He has made me aware of areas in my life that I've overlooked. A selfish motive here or an overlooked sin there. This regular habit of asking God for forgiveness has allowed me to have a daily reset. It's a constant habit of drawing near to God, believing that slowly but surely, I am becoming more and more like Jesus through the habit of looking to Him for help with my sinful heart. A heart, like yours, that God waits for and longs to have come home to Him.

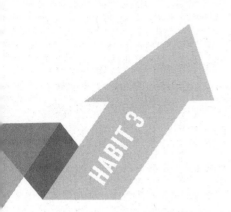

Talk to God

WHEN I WAS FOUR YEARS OLD, I asked my dad where he stored his shaving cream. When he asked me why I wanted to know, I told him it was because my beard needed a trim. This would be funnier if you knew what I look like today. I'm currently twenty-seven years old, and I can say quite confidently that my beard has never needed a trim. Facial hair isn't exactly a gift that I've been given.

My dad, on the other hand, has always been able to grow a pretty decent beard. As a little kid, I would watch him every morning walk into the bathroom, get out his single blade razor, fumble through the drawer for some shaving cream, and begin shaving. It was something he did every single day.

I've always looked up to my dad. He is a great man. He has a continual love for the Lord, he raised me to love Him, and he has been an amazing dad to me. When I was little, I didn't just look up to him, I thought he was an

53

actual superhero. I couldn't believe how strong he was. He could pick up my toy rocking horse all by himself. I couldn't believe how high he could jump. Sometimes in the driveway, he could even jump up and touch the rim of our basketball hoop. And I couldn't believe how much food he could eat. Sometimes he could take out an entire box of Cinnamon Toast Crunch in one sitting. Yeah, I wanted to be like that. I wanted to be just like him. At four years old, I tried to figure out the source of his superpowers. One of my first guesses was his daily morning shave.

My mom actually has a picture of my first shave. My dad let me put shaving cream all over my face (some ended up in my hair—it was awesome) and then remove it all with the cap of a ballpoint pen. I had no idea that pen caps weren't the same as razor blades. I had no idea I wasn't removing hair from my face. I didn't know that I would (probably) never be able to grow a beard like the guys in the Old Spice commercials. All I knew was that my dad shaved every day and I thought my dad was The Man. So if Dad shaved, I should do it, too. Maybe shaving was the secret to his powers.

There is something about people we look up to that goes beyond just being in awe of them—we want to know all about them. Why are they so great? What is their secret sauce? What are their habits? What do they do when nobody is looking so that when everyone is, greatness is obvious? We want to know where their superpower comes from.

We see this same phenomenon with Jesus and His disciples. They didn't just think Jesus was The Man, they knew it. They watched Him heal the sick, multiply a boy's sack lunch into an all-you-can-eat buffet, and even raise Lazarus from the dead. They knew if there was ever somebody to try to be like, it was this Jesus guy.

The disciples spent every single day with Him, and they knew He was the real deal. They walked with Him. They talked with Him. They ate lunch with Him. They got to see His routines. They watched who He talked to, and about what. The disciples had a front-row view into the life of Jesus.

In Luke 11, the disciples ask Jesus an extremely important and revealing question. It was their "Where do you keep your shaving cream?" moment. They believed they had figured out the core of what made Jesus so different. They believed that they had found His most important habit, His superpower: "Lord, teach us to pray" (Luke 11:1).

There is so much we can take from this. There were plenty of people in those days who were good at prayer. The disciples themselves likely prayed regularly. And yet they wanted to sit in front of Jesus and take notes on how to pray, because in comparison to the prayers of Jesus, they didn't even think they knew how.

The disciples had seen, and would continue to see, Jesus praying often. He prayed by Himself (Luke 5:16). He prayed in front of others (Luke 9:28). He prayed when in celebration (Luke 3:21). He prayed when in pain (Matthew 27:46). He prayed during stressful times (Matthew 4). He prayed when in need (Luke 22:40). He prayed for the disciples (John 17:6). He prayed for all believers (John

17:20). He prayed before doing miracles (John 11:4). He was always praying.

For Jesus, prayer was not the spare tire—it was His steering wheel. It was not the last resort; it was what He went to first! For many people, prayer is need based. For Jesus, the need was to pray.

We see prayer as a central habit throughout the Bible. For Jesus and many others, prayer was not just a habit in their life, prayer *was* their life. Daniel had more insight and influence from his prayer closet than the king did from his throne (see Daniel 2). Hannah prayed for a son, and was granted one who would become a prophet to all of Israel. Jonah prayed, in possibly the most disgusting place of all time. Moses prayed and a sea split in two. Elijah prayed and fire fell from the sky. Paul prayed in a prison and the entire foundation shook. Prayer supplied power for their lives and can supply power in yours, too.

Evangelist and author Leonard Ravenhill once said: "The pastor who is not praying is playing."[1] He was warning that a sermon that isn't covered in prayer is a sermon that is missing out on real power.

It is true of all believers: The Christian who is not praying is playing. If your life is not covered in prayer, your life is missing out on real power. We cannot live fruitfully if we do not also live prayerfully.

If you long for greater intimacy with Jesus, try prayer. If you long to make a greater impact on the world, try prayer. If you just need a change, let prayer be that change. Let talking to God be your superpower. It has power like nothing else to change three major areas: things, people, and me.

1. Prayer changes things

The people who pray the greatest prayers are not people who are the best with words. The greatest prayers are from people who have the greatest belief. They pray believing. Prayer without belief is just a wish. Prayer with belief is powerful.

There is a massive difference between worrying in your mind and calling it prayer, and actually opening up your mouth and talking to God as if He hears you and wants to answer your prayers.

As we pray believing for things to change, what we are actually doing is having faith that God hears us and will change what we are praying for. Faith is the secret sauce to our prayers. Hebrews 11:6 tells us that it is impossible to please God without faith. If we can't please God without faith, we definitely shouldn't pray to God without faith. When you pray, do you truly believe that your prayers are making a difference?

Paul put it this way, "For we are God's fellow workers; you are God's field, you are God's building" (1 Corinthians 3:9 NKJV). Paul is actually saying that we get to work together with God to determine outcomes. Let me say that again: *You can work together with God to determine outcomes!*

For a long time I believed my prayers would only be answered if they were in line with God's predetermined will. I would pray, not fully believing that anything would change unless I happened to be praying a prayer that was in line with God's preplanned will. It was almost like

There is a massive difference between worrying in your mind and calling it prayer, and actually opening up your mouth and talking to God as if He hears you and wants to answer your prayers.

playing hangman, hoping that my prayer would fill in the right blanks.

But when we look at the Bible, the best prayer manual on the planet, we see that throughout Scripture, God is actually *moved* by the prayers of His people. Your prayers actually change things because your prayers can move God to change them.

Let this idea about prayer change everything about your prayer life. Instead of prayer being a defensive strategy, take your prayers on the offensive. When things aren't going your way, don't adjust your prayers and back off. Continue to pray and believe that God *is* going to change things. When you are praying for a miracle and it doesn't happen on your timeline, don't just assume that it's not the will of God. Pray and believe that the miracle is going to happen *today*.

Don't let things change your prayer life, let your prayer life change things.

2. Prayer changes people

E. M. Bounds is widely recognized as one of the greatest authors ever on the subject of prayer. He lived in the 1800s and early 1900s, and is rumored to have spent hours a day in fervent prayer. A few years ago, I came across his most famous prayer book, *Power through Prayer*, and could not put it down. I highly recommend it. It is filled with deep insights and revelation on the superpower of prayer. My favorite quote from the book: "Talking to men for God is a great thing, but talking to God for men is greater still."[2]

E. M. Bounds believed that praying for other people is the most effective way to see them changed.

He wasn't alone in that belief. Leonard Ravenhill said, "The man who can get believers to praying would, under God, usher in the greatest revival that the world has ever known."[3] Notice these two men of great faith did not say revival would come when our preaching gets better. They said revival will come when our praying gets better.

I'll be honest with you. I haven't actually been the best at praying for people. When someone asks for prayer, I always say I will. But it doesn't always happen. When something bad happens in the world, I typically share on social media that I am going to pray. But many times, I don't actually pray.

When is the last time you actually prayed for someone outside of your immediate circle of friends and family? When is the last time you prayed for the lost?

I recently met a high school student I'll call Luke. Luke was invited to church for the first time when he was fifteen years old. The very first time he went to a youth service, he gave his life to Christ. Luke never missed youth group after that. When the church doors were open, he was there. Sunday mornings, Wednesday nights, Thursday afternoons, it didn't matter. He wanted to be at church learning about Jesus, even if it meant he was alone.

No one else in Luke's family was a follower of Jesus. Luke invited his siblings multiple times, but they never came. When Luke invited his parents, they told him they had no desire to go with him. Every week Luke would sit in church with his friend's family, wishing he was sitting with his.

Then one day Luke's pastor preached a sermon on prayer. Luke started waking up thirty minutes earlier to pray for his family. Every day he would pray that they would come to know Jesus. He began to come down to the altar at the end of church services and spend time in prayer for them there.

Three months went by and nothing changed. But he kept praying.

Six months passed and nothing changed. But he kept praying. A year came and went, and he was still sitting by himself. But he kept on praying. Finally, after fifteen months of praying every day, Luke's parents showed up in church on Sunday. Would it surprise you if I told you Luke's entire family now follows Jesus? It's true. Luke's prayers worked.

I had heard about Luke from his youth pastor and was blown away by his faith. When I met him and talked to him in person, I was even more blown away. I asked him what his prayer life looks like now. This is what he said:

> It hasn't changed. I've been getting up every morning for thirty minutes to pray specifically for the lost people in my life. I'm so happy my family knows Jesus, but I've still got a lot of praying to do. If God can do it for them, I believe He will do it for my new list of people I'm praying for, too.

Luke gets it. Prayer changes people. Will you pray?

3. Prayer changes you

Perhaps the most underrated and life-changing part of prayer is how much it changes the person who is actually doing the praying. You can start praying for a situation and end up realizing you are actually the one who needs to change. You can begin your prayer time for others and end up being the one who is radically changed by the presence of God.

One of the great discouragements for people who are new to praying is when they have faith for God to answer their prayer, and He does not. It can seem like they're praying the wrong way. I've watched it over and over: People who desire to have a great prayer life suddenly give up on prayer when it seems like God goes silent. This is a huge mistake.

If a mechanic tried to turn on his car and it wouldn't start, he wouldn't throw the car away. He would first make sure it wasn't out of gas. Then he would tow it to the garage and open up the hood. He would get under it and assess the situation. He would get the right parts needed for the job. He would *keep going* until he found answers.

Persevering in prayer is never a waste of time. To me, that's the coolest part about prayer. That even when things and people don't change, I am always being changed through my praying.

Prayer is actively inviting God into your day. It's a decision to give God your attention as you speak to Him. Giving your attention to God is never a waste of time.

Through our prayers, we are becoming more and more like God Himself.

When we give God our attention, God gives us His perspective. It may be that nothing about your situation will change. But something even better might change when you pray: *you*.

HABIT: THE 1-MINUTE PRAYER

Do you have someone you text off and on all day? Maybe it's a spouse or a boyfriend or girlfriend. Perhaps it is a best friend or a co-worker. This is a person you trust. You talk about shared passions. You aren't afraid to text them late at night or early in the morning because you know they'll answer. You definitely have sent each other a meme or two.

I think God desires our prayer life with Him to be pretty similar to our communication with that friend. I think He wants to talk a lot. I think He wants no subject or time of the day to be off limits. I don't think He wants it to all be serious either; in fact, I think He wants to laugh with you.

In 1 Thessalonians 5:17, Paul encourages us to "pray continually."

It used to be that every time I heard that verse, I would get very anxious. Because praying without ceasing intimidated me. How was I possibly supposed to do that while in college, working two different jobs, trying to balance the relationships in my life, and somehow keep up with my beloved Boston Celtics?

Not only did constant prayer intimidate me, but since I am being honest, the thought of it bored me. I didn't know how to talk to God that long. I didn't know what to talk to Him about, even. I heard stories of people at church who would wake up hours before work to pray and I just assumed they loved God way more than I did.

But I knew I needed to pray. In fact, I desired to pray more. I just didn't quite know where to start. *Then the 1-minute prayer entered the chat.* The 1-minute prayer is a simple way for anyone to build up the habit of talking to God consistently throughout the day. Anyone! It's quite simple. Here's how it works.

Let's say your schedule today looks exactly like mine:

5:30 a.m. wake up

5:40 a.m. Bible time

6:15 a.m. workout

7:00 a.m. get ready for the day

8:00 a.m. spend time with son and wife

8:45 a.m. leave for work

9:00 a.m. staff meeting

11:00 a.m. phone call with board member

Noon lunch with a friend

1:00 p.m. study time

3:00 p.m. Zoom call with pastors in Nashville

4:00 p.m. wrap up work/emails

5:00 p.m. arrive home

6:00 p.m. dinner with family

7:00 p.m. play with son

8:00 p.m. intentional time with wife

9:30 p.m. bed

Now, for me, that is a pretty full day. But I *know* my prayer life is going to be unaffected by busyness because of the 1-minute prayer. Basically, after every event or activity throughout my day, I stop for one minute to talk to God before I move on to the next thing on my calendar. That's it! It's that simple, and it allows me to have a constant conversation with God throughout the day.

"Well, what do you pray for one minute?" I'm glad you asked. The answer is *anything* and the answer is *everything*. Here are a few possible examples of prayer from my day.

After workout:

God, thank You for another day. Thank You for the health You've given me to even be working out today. I know I don't look like Michael B. Jordan yet, but I know that even when I don't see it, You're working.

I told you. I'm a firm believer that God enjoys humor.

After leaving for work:

Hey, God. Me again. I'm heading to staff meeting, and I really feel like at the beginning of the meeting today I'm supposed to challenge them with the same challenge You've been speaking to me about. Can You give me the words and the wisdom to do that in a way that is encouraging and unifying? I love these people like family, and I want what happens today to be a reflection of that. Thank You for Your presence.

After having lunch with a friend:

What a blessing friends are, Lord. I know you already know what is going on in his life and you know all about the things he just shared with me . . . but I told my friend I would pray for him, so I'd like to do that now. Lord, please touch my friend. Give him discernment in this situation. Let him know he is not alone. He has friends who care about him deeply and a God who cares even more. I pray that even now on his car ride home, he would be reminded of those things and believe them. In Jesus' name, Amen.

Before heading home after work:

What an awesome day. Thank You, Jesus, for all that You did at work today. I'm so excited I get to spend the rest of the day with You and my beautiful family. Help me to leave work at work so I can be present with Maddy and Lion the rest of the night. Help me to be the dad that You've called me to be even for these next few hours. Amen.

Constant communication, like texting that friend. The convo changes throughout the day. Sometimes it's serious and requires asking for things, other times it's a meme fest and filled with laughter. The takeaway is this: Talking to God is your superpower. It changes things, people, and you. It grows your relationship with God in a way that few other things can.

Your prayer life can be consistent and powerful. I believe that even the newest of pray-ers will find that as you pray, you will not only get better at it but you will fall in love with it. Talking to God is worth it.

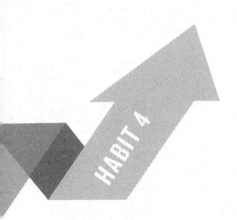

HABIT 4

Rest So You Can Run

THE GOAL OF THE FIRST FEW PAGES of this chapter is to make you deeply and provocatively jealous. *Jealous.* Let me describe to you what last Friday looked like for me, from the time I woke up until the time I went to bed.

I didn't set an alarm. My wife and I simply woke up when the sun told us to. When the room was filled with sunlight, we rolled out of bed and went downstairs. I walked into the kitchen and turned on my favorite John Mayer playlist through our Bluetooth speaker. While Maddy was feeding Lion, I made our favorite pour-over coffee, a single origin blend from Guatemala. Then I made a delicious breakfast of egg whites, blueberries, and black-peppered bacon with syrup and brown sugar drizzled over the top. Delicious. As we ate, we spent a few minutes reading our Bibles, the only noise coming from our son, Lion, laughing as he played with our dog Mogley on the floor.

After thoroughly enjoying breakfast, we put Lion in his stroller and went for a slow walk around our neighborhood. The walk wasn't for exercise—we had no agenda other than enjoying each other's company and being outside in the beautiful, sixty-five-degree, light autumn air. We talked about what happened on the latest episode of our favorite TV show, we laughed at our son waving to someone's dog down the street, and we talked about our hopes for the season that we are in as pastors. When our walk was over, we went inside and put Lion down for a nap so that we could get ready for the day.

When he was awake again, we hopped in the car and headed to an outdoor shopping area. We walked around, wandering in and out of a few of our favorite stores. Maddy bought a new beanie for herself, I found a new retro-looking coffee mug to add to our collection, and Lion waved and laughed from his stroller at every new stranger that he saw. We ended our shopping trip by eating a light lunch together. Lion thoroughly enjoyed the little bit of chocolate chip cookie we gave him.

By the time we got back home, it was about one o'clock. Maddy sat outside on our porch and read from her new favorite book while Lion played in the yard. I decided to "rest my eyes" and took an hour nap on the couch. (Yeah, a nap. Jealous yet?). When I woke up, it was about time for Lion to take his second nap. Maddy said she was going to continue reading her book, so I grabbed my golf clubs and went to the driving range near our house to hit a few golf balls. I met a nice guy named Dan and we talked about our families, our jobs, and the Tennessee Titans. After about an hour or so of doing one of my favorite things, I returned home, and Maddy reminded me that we were doing dinner with friends. I showered, and the three of us headed to our favorite sushi restaurant for an early dinner with some of our best friends. We shared several rolls of sushi and an appetizer of salmon belly nigiri. It was heavenly. We didn't rush, and we laughed a lot. After dinner, we walked across the street and got ice cream at Jeni's Splendid Ice Creams. I got a waffle cone with two scoops of salted caramel with peanut butter chunks. Out. Of. This. World.

When we got home, we put Lion to bed, and Maddy and I sat down to enjoy each other's company, uninterrupted. We played a card game called Monopoly Deal. Maddy won. Then we watched our favorite stand-up comedian in his new Netflix special. Around ten o'clock, pretty worn out from our incredible time together, we went to sleep. Ending a full day of our favorite things and our favorite people.

Well? Were you jealous at all? What if I told you that we do a day similar to this every single week—where we just have fun, enjoy each other's company, and rest? Would that make you even more jealous? What if I told you that this is actually something God wants for you? That you were *made* to sabbath, or rest?

We see the holy rhythm of sabbath from the very beginning of creation. God spends six incredible days creating what you and I see as planet Earth and everything that's on it. But on the seventh day, God stops creating altogether.

By the seventh day God had finished the work he had been doing; so on the seventh day he rested from all his work. Then God blessed the seventh day and made it holy, because on it he rested from all the work of creating that he had done.

Genesis 2:2–3

God, from the beginning, modeled the way our week should look.

By the time we get from the book of Genesis to the book of Exodus, however, the Sabbath was no longer a possibility for God's people. The Israelites had become slaves in Egypt, and Pharaoh was quite literally a slave driver. There was no time for pleasure or family or delighting in anything. Life was about how much you could produce. A few hours away from your job post would likely be a death sentence. There was no way you could take an entire day off.

God, who is always faithful to His people, sent the Israelites a leader named Moses who guided the Israelites out of Egypt in pretty epic fashion. If you've never read the story, you should. There are fist fights, wild toads, hail storms, wooden staffs turning into snakes, water turning into blood, an entire sea splitting into two, and that is just the beginning. The end result of the story is that the Israelites witness the power of God to set them free, after more than four hundred years. God is faithful.

One of the first things God did when His people were free was to give their leader Moses instructions on how they were to live. Here was one of those instructions:

> Remember the Sabbath day by keeping it holy. Six days you shall labor and do all your work, but the seventh day is a sabbath to the LORD your God. On it you shall not do any work, neither you, nor your son or daughter, nor your male or female servant, nor your animals, nor any foreigner residing in your towns.
>
> Exodus 20:8–10

This particular instruction from the Lord was received in celebration by the Israelites. No work? For anyone? All day? It was such a massive contrast to their reality in Egypt that it was probably hard to even process what a weekly day off would look like. But the Sabbath was even greater than a day of no production; it was a deemed a "holy" day.

The world *holy*, especially in the Western world, has somehow gained a connotation that is not accurate in the slightest. As you read this, you may hear the word *holy* and think of a very religious and pretentious kid you grew up with in church. Perhaps you hear the word *holy* and think about rules and regulations that hamper your life. Maybe you think about the way your parents used to make you dress for Sunday morning church. But have you ever thought about what the word *holy* actually means?

Holy, in its proper context, is one of the most beautiful words. It means "to be set apart" or "to be sacred." It's a word used over six hundred times in the Bible. *Holy* is the word used by the angels as they sing to God. When heard by the Israelites a few thousand years ago, the word *holy* would have been even more exciting than the phrase *weekly day off*. It was a word reserved for the highest

73

honor. They didn't use the word *holy* flippantly. It was used only to describe the things of God or God Himself, which was the pursuit of their entire lives. The words *sabbath* and *holy* in the same sentence would bring almost too much joy to bear. A special, sacred, pleasure-filled, delighting, and holy day off? Every single week? Pure bliss.

A lot has changed in the world since the Israelites celebrated the gift of sabbath. In America, a day off in general is now a sign of weakness. Producing and becoming something better and greater have become gods. Phrases like "I'll sleep when I'm dead" and "I'm gonna make it no matter what" and "I'm always grinding" are celebrated and repeated like a verbal badge of honor in a culture where work now defines identity.

Today, people who overwork themselves are seen as heroes. Two thousand years ago, people who overworked were called slaves. God wants you to be free.

Sabbath keeps us free from the shackles of achievement and production. It is not just freedom from producing. Sabbath is freedom from producing something of ourselves. It's the act of intentionally doing nothing to earn the love of God while accepting the fact that He could not love you any more than He already does. We find the freedom to move from being productive to being present.

Being present is not possible when fear is a part of the equation. Satan knows this, which is why he tries to persuade us that we are missing out when we pause for an entire day. His plan has always been to try to convince us that we should seek blessings without God. He twists God's words and tries to get us to question if God really always has our best interest in mind.

Will stopping for an entire day really help you?

The person you're up against for the promotion is probably working today.

Imagine how much better your life would be if you just sacrificed sabbath for a season.

Lies.

The reality is this: Never resting doesn't accelerate the work of God in our life. It corrupts it. When we don't live according to God's example and design, we find ourselves living at a pace that God hasn't blessed. It could lead to full bank accounts, but empty souls. To success at the expense of peace.

On the contrary, when we stop once a week to observe the Sabbath, we live all seven days differently. A person who is rested produces better, interacts better, and ultimately loves better. Sabbath is not hindering you, it is helping you.

One of the things I've observed in the lives of many Christians I know who haven't practiced the habit of taking sabbath is the reality of burnout. They are on fire for Jesus, they are serving Him in amazing ways, they are a light to their co-workers, but time passes and the fire that was once alive turns into an ember. People who once were leading the charge at church barely attend. Others with all the talent in the world had to be removed from leadership because their souls were crumbling. You probably are familiar with similar stories. It's heartbreaking.

Never resting doesn't accelerate the work of God in our life. It corrupts it. When we don't live according to God's example and design, we find ourselves living at a pace that God hasn't blessed.

One of the most well-known illustrations in the Bible used to describe the life of a believer is that of running a race. I've participated in a few races in my life, and usually the winner of the race is not the one who starts out in the lead. The winners of most races are strategically and intentionally pacing themselves so that at the finish line they are not running out of gas but finishing strong.

God doesn't just want you to start well, He wants you to finish well. The Bible actually has a word for people who finish their race well: faithful. Our goal as followers of Jesus should be that we are faithful finishers of what God has asked us to do. Sabbath is one of the best strategies for finishing. If you don't rest well, you won't run long. When you rest well, you can persevere. You can pace yourself and thrive according to God's plan. You can operate from a place of overflow. You can do more with less time. You can enjoy life again.

Is your soul weary? Are you tired? Are you burned out from a rhythm of life that you've been trying to sustain on your own? Maybe it's time to try the rhythm God designed for you. One that includes a weekly sabbath.

Imagine that you were alive one thousand years ago. You have a family, a small house you are thankful for, and a job you enjoy. Your job is to build tables, and you build great ones. In fact, you are known for the quality of your work in your little town. Having one of your tables is a status booster.

You eventually get a job offer from the king of the kingdom himself. You are now one of the few people in the world who make tables for the royal magistrates and other important people of the kingdom. What an honor. Your tables are used in beautiful homes, important government buildings, and everywhere in between.

One day, you are in your garage making the newest table requested of you: a long mahogany that will be used in one of the king's conference rooms. All of a sudden, the doorbell rings. You are a little frustrated, not wanting to leave your work, but you take your gloves off and head to the door. When you open it, you are shocked.

There, standing in *your* doorway is the king. Your jaw hits the floor. This was the last thing you were expecting. You wonder, *Am I wearing deodorant?* Never mind, too late for that. The king asks if he can come inside. He tells you that he's heard a lot about you and that he's cleared his entire schedule to come and be with you today. *What?*

Now, imagine how crazy it would if you turned to the king and said, "I'm so sorry, king. I just don't have time for that today. I'm making a very important table in the garage."

"Hmm. Who is the table for?" the king asks.

"Well, it's technically for . . . you," you reply.

"I see. Could you maybe pause for the day and go back to it tomorrow? I think your boss would probably be okay with that," the king says, smiling.

"Oh no, I don't think I could do that," you reply. "People expect the best from me, you see. I have a reputation!"

Do you see how crazy this would be? Of course you wouldn't do this. You would drop everything you had planned that day to simply be with the king. Because being with the king is more important than working for the king.

You are someone who the King desires to spend time with. You are someone who the true King was willing to lay His life down for, so that one day you would be willing to be present with Him. Sabbath is being with your King. It's pausing, knowing that your value is not found in what you do, but in who you are. It's an entire day where you get to simply *be* and not worry about producing. Twenty-four hours of living the dream.

So, how exactly do you sabbath? Let's start with what it's not.

What sabbath is not:

- It is not just a day off.
- It's not a day of hibernation where you just sleep all day (although naps are welcome).
- It's not the day you do all the extra stuff you didn't get done earlier in the week.
- It's not a Netflix marathon day.

What sabbath is:

- A pause from the regularly scheduled program.
- A time where you rest, worship, or delight *only*. If the activity doesn't fit in rest, worship, or delight, you save it for another day of the week—you have six others to choose from.

- A full 24-hour period observed once a week.
- A rhythm of life that you get better at as you do it.

HABIT: TAKE A DAY TO REST

Pick a day—any day of the week will work. Traditionally for the Jewish people, their sabbath took place starting at sundown on Friday and lasted until sundown on Saturday.

Many who practice sabbath in America do so from Saturday evening to Sunday evening. My wife and I do Thursday evening to Friday evening due to our weekends normally being work times. The point is that the Sabbath was made for you (Mark 2:27), so practice it on a day that makes the most sense in your life, one that can be kept regularly.

After you have your day picked out, clear your calendar. Then ask yourself: What could I do during these twenty-four hours that would bring me joy and delight and allow me to be refreshed for the next six days? It's a fun question. Your answers will probably change over time, so keep careful track of what the most life-giving things are in your life.

Here are a few of my favorite things to do on sabbath, as an example:

- golf
- drink good coffee
- play games with my family

- go for a walk
- read
- listen to worship music
- grill out
- go swimming
- have friends over
- eat really good food
- buy my wife flowers
- play basketball

My wife's list has some of these, but many are different. If you're single, picking out things to do on sabbath is pretty straightforward. Just do what gives you life. If you're married, work as a team to make sure you both are doing things you love. Sabbath isn't a day for one spouse to have the best day and the other to have the worst. It should be a great day for you both and it will take communication to make sure it is.

Waking up the day your sabbath begins should be like waking up as a little kid on Christmas morning. If it's not, then you are doing sabbath wrong. Every week our family looks forward to our sabbath with eager joy. We love and cherish that time deeply. A good sabbath should bring forth the same emotion in you.

Keep it this simple:

1. Pick a day.
2. Pick your activities.
3. Worship God.

4. Enjoy the life He's given you.

5. Allow your soul to fill back up.

Just remember: Sabbath was made for you, not you for sabbath. This habit is not a to-do list, it's a blessing. A gift from God. Receive this amazing gift He gives you. Now, go rest so that you can run!

Keep It Simple

PEOPLE HAVE LOOKED EVERYWHERE FOR IT. Romantics around the world have spent millions seeking it. Individuals have dreamed their entire lives of finding it. Finally, I, Noah Herrin, have found the secret to a great marriage: food.

I am one thousand percent convinced that food is the secret to love. If you are in a new relationship, have been dating for a while, or are married and you don't believe me, I dare you to cook a meal for your significant other and see what happens.

The other day I was in need of some brownie points, I won't lie. This happens from time to time. I don't want to go into all of the details, but my sarcastic mouth had gotten me into some trouble. So I went on YouTube and looked up how to cook some *bomb* chicken alfredo (shout out to YouTube University).

When my wife got home that evening, there was chicken alfredo already on the table. There was Texas toast in the oven and the aroma of love in the air.

You would have thought we were back on our honeymoon. My wife was absolutely googly-eyed at me. Honestly, I could hardly even taste the pasta because she kept trying to kiss me and stuff. I was like, *Wow! Food is the secret!* I looked at her and said, "You want me to cook some brownies later or something?"

But in the same way that food is the secret to love, I am also convinced that it starts more arguments than anything. What I'm about to describe to you has happened many times.

Every week or so, we go out to a restaurant for date night. I show up hungry, because if I'm going to spend money on good food I want to make it worth it. So when the waiter or waitress asks us what we want to eat, I tell them I want the big bacon burger with sweet potato fries, and not to hold back on the fries. But then my wife Maddy will say something like this.

"Umm. You know, I'm not really that hungry. I think I'll just have a Caesar side salad, please."

My response is typically to smile at the waiter or waitress, and say, "Excuse me, let me have a quick word with my beautiful wife. . . . Umm, babe, side salad? Are you sure that's all you want for dinner?"

"Yes. A side salad sounds great," Maddy will say.

"Are you positive?" I'll ask again. "Because I'm really hungry, and the burgers at this place are out of this world. I just don't want you getting jealous when you

see my food come out. You know how I feel about shar-
ing food. . . ."

"I just want the side salad," Maddy will repeat.

Twenty minutes later, the waiter walks out with a tray
in his hand. He sets my plate in front of me. A mouthwa-
tering burger with two patties, cheddar cheese, and two
thick-cut pieces of bacon on top, paired with a mound
of sweet potato fries that look like they were delivered
straight from heaven. Then he places a tiny little plate of
lettuce and Caesar dressing in front of Maddy.

About two minutes into dinner, Maddy grows elastic
arms and tries to take one of my sweet potato fries. I have
seen this move before, so I'm prepared. I karate chop her
arm away from the fry.

Maddy says, "Are you serious right now? Did you just
karate chop my arm away from a french fry?"

"You said you weren't hungry."

"I just wanted to try a french fry!"

"I warned you this would happen."

"Jeez. I didn't know you were so emotionally attached
to that french fry. Are you guys in a relationship or something? Is it Facebook official?"

I continue eating.

"I would have let you eat some of my salad if you had
asked me."

"I don't want your romaine, which is why I didn't order
it."

The point: Food is a blessing and it is a curse. One
of my favorite commercials is for Snickers candy bars:
"You're not you when you're hungry." It's funny, because

it's true. We sometimes do and say things we don't mean when we are hungry.

Becoming hungry is normal. If you go long enough without eating, eventually your stomach is going to start speaking to you. It's just how we are made to operate.

Spiritual hunger is normal, too. Eventually, all of us begin to crave something to fill us up spiritually. In those moments of hunger, what we eat can either change our lives for the better or absolutely destroy us. Here's the truth: Every single one of us will get spiritually hungry, but not all of us will become full.

Jesus understood that we would have to wrestle with our spiritual hunger, and He offered some advice to help save us from eating the wrong things when He said, "I am the bread of life. Whoever comes to me will never go hungry, and whoever believes in me will never be thirsty" (John 6:35).

Jesus was speaking directly to people, much like us, who were spiritually hungry, trying to get full from something temporary and insignificant.

The day before Jesus said this, earlier in John 6, these people were sitting on a hillside listening to Jesus talk about the Kingdom of God. Time passed and they grew hungry, but there was a huge problem. Only one out of thousands of them had remembered to pack a lunch— just one! A young boy brought his fish sticks and garlic bread over to Jesus, and Jesus did a very Jesus thing. He multiplied the food so that a few bites turned into an all-you-can-eat buffet for thousands of people. A true miracle.

The next day, the buffet people (can we call them that?) follow Jesus to the other side of the lake. We learn through Jesus (in John 6:26) that they've followed Him not because they wanted more of Him, but because they craved more bread. They were hungry for the wrong thing. They were standing right in front of the Bread of Life Himself, but all they could see was another free meal.

Isn't it interesting that most of the time, gods (idols) start out as gifts?

Maybe God gives you a good gift, like a platform. He blesses you with more influence than you know what to do with. In the beginning, you use this gift to give God glory and to make His name known. Until the day your followers go left and God goes right. And instead of going with God, you go with your followers because you don't want to lose them. All of a sudden a gift has turned into a god. Influence has become an idol.

Maybe God gives you a good gift, like money. You start using the money to bless others and to build God's church and live generously for His Kingdom. But the day comes when you go from dreaming about how to bless others to dreaming about how to bless yourself. Instead of you using money, money starts using you. A gift, slowly but surely, turns into a god.

Maybe God gives you a good gift, like a ministry. You are a great ministry leader. You love serving people and reaching the lost. But somewhere along the way, you fall more in love with working *for* Jesus than being *with* Jesus. And once again, a gift turns into a god.

Take note of what your cravings are. Be careful to recognize when your appetite changes. Temporary things will never satisfy you eternally. Jesus said "I *am* the bread of life." Only He can truly fill you up. Zacchaeus tried the Bread of Life, and gave half of everything he owned to the poor (see Luke 19). Peter tried the Bread of Life, and said, in effect, "Lord, where else would I possibly go?" (see John 6:68). David tried the Bread of Life and danced before the Lord. Paul tried the Bread of Life and went from being a disciple killer to a disciple maker. The thief on the cross tried the Bread of Life and later that day was with Jesus in paradise.

Are you hungry? There is only one person who will truly fill you. His name is Jesus.

Jesus addresses the topic of hunger in many ways throughout the gospels. One of His most well-known teachings is in Matthew, "For where your treasure is, there your heart will be also" (6:21).

In other words, what you value the most will end up being what you continue to hunger for. When you eat something long enough, you eventually develop an appetite for more. You crave what you repeatedly eat.

Matthew 6:21 is most often quoted in discussions about money. Treasure is typically attached to some sort of monetary value, after all. But there is one thing more valuable than dollars, and that is time. It is our most valuable resource. How we spend our time is an indication of what we treasure most.

Where do you spend your time? Today, people are spending a lot of time on their phones. According to a study done by Statista, almost half of all American are spending five to six hours a day on their smart device.[1] This study was done on a broad range of age groups. We can only imagine that the five to six hours a day would be even higher if the study had been conducted solely on the younger generation.

Great author and pastor John Piper said this: "One of the great uses of Twitter and Facebook will be to prove at the Last Day that prayerlessness was not from lack of time."[2] That made me want to throw my phone away. Talk about conviction.

Your iPhone or Android is not, by itself, dangerous to the Christian life. It is distracting, but not dangerous. What is found on your iPhone—that is another story altogether. That can be very dangerous!

At the risk of sounding like I am an anti-technology conspiracy theorist, let me just cut to the chase. Social media is doing a lot to us, and most of it is not positive. What we look at when we open our social media apps is called a "feed"—what you eat, or "feed" on, matters. If you are continually "eating" comparison, eventually you will become someone whose natural reaction is to compare. If you are constantly looking at people who seem to have more, you are eventually going to crave more. If you are consuming lustful photos, eventually you will crave lust in relationships.

The solution to all of this hunger stuff is twofold.

1. Hunger for Jesus: He alone will satisfy us. Even when we know this as truth, we have to *constantly*

remind ourselves that everything else will ultimately leave us empty.

2. Actively fight to be content.

One of the verses in the Bible that seems to be taken out of context most often is Philippians 4:13. Many people use this verse as motivation to defeat whatever obstacle or opponent they find in front of them. But it isn't about courageous victory over enemies. It's about courageous victory over self and the need for more. Look at the verse in context, written by Paul when he was in prison:

> I know what it is to be in need, and I know what it is to have plenty. I have learned the secret of being content in any and every situation, whether well fed or hungry, whether living in plenty or in want. I can do all things through him who gives me strength.
>
> Philippians 4:12–13

Paul boasts that he can do *all* things through Christ who gives him strength. But he is not boasting about accomplishing great things. He is boasting that he no longer needs to have things to be satisfied: "I have learned the secret of being content in any and every situation."

Would you describe yourself as content? The definition of the word *content* is "the state of being satisfied. Having peaceful joy." Sometimes I am content. If I'm being honest, many times I am not content. I've been tracking my contentment levels a lot lately. What I've found is that being content is a daily fight, and that the environment I'm in directly affects my ability to win or lose the fight.

When I'm in certain environments where I'm tempted over and over again to pursue the wrong thing, it's harder for me to win the battle of being content. For instance, when I am around ambitious people who have very little desire to build the Kingdom of God and a very intense desire to build the kingdom of self, they rub off on me. But when I'm surrounded by others who are also pursuing contentment in Christ, the battle is easier. That doesn't mean we shouldn't have goals for ourselves or want to see healthy growth. It simply means that our contentment isn't dependent on those things, but on Jesus. The more we practice, the easier it is for us to truly be content.

The next habit is one that helps put us in the right place to crave the right thing: Jesus. It's a habit that will hopefully limit the amount of time you spend in environments that encourage the desire for more of the wrong things. It is all about keeping it simple.

HABIT: KEEP IT SIMPLE

I want to help you develop the habit of running everything you do, everything you spend, and everything you pursue through a life filter. The filter is a *simple* one. It involves asking yourself, Does this help me seek God's kingdom first? (See Matthew 6:25.)

Many people have a misconception about the Kingdom of God. They subconsciously believe that when we get saved, we are all waiting around to die so that we can enter heaven and experience the Kingdom of God. No, we are not waiting around to get into the Kingdom of God; God is actively trying to get the Kingdom of God into us *now*. The more we live in His Kingdom, the more we will desire of it.

Remember: Whatever you eat consistently will be what you crave consistently. Jesus said to "seek first his kingdom and his righteousness, and all these things will be given to you as well" (Matthew 6:33). Richard Foster said, "The person who does not seek the kingdom first doesn't seek it at all."[3] When we run our decisions through that filter first, it helps us keep God first.

This habit, admittedly, will be one of the hardest ones. It goes against everything our culture tells us. The world we live in says, "Do what you want, buy what you want, and pursue every dream that you have." Jesus came with a very different message of "Resist your flesh, sell everything you have and give it to the poor, and take up your cross." One seeks the kingdom of me; the other seeks the Kingdom of God. One leaves us empty at night; the other leaves us full. The kingdom of me will leave us horribly let down. The Kingdom of God will leave us completely and utterly satisfied.

This habit covers three areas:

1. Everything we do (time)
2. Everything we spend (money)
3. Everything we pursue (dream)

Whatever you eat consistently will be what you crave consistently. Jesus said to "seek first his kingdom and his righteousness, and all these things will be given to you as well" (Matthew 6:33).

1. Everything we do

If you want to see where a person's heart is, look at how they spend their time. Maybe you spend ten hours a day at work, and are thinking to yourself, *Well that's not fair! I have to go to work.* Absolutely. Bills have to be paid, I get it.

What I'm talking about is not what you absolutely have to do, but what you get to do. How do you spend your free time? Do you spend the time outside of work on things that are going to last eternally? Do you prioritize godly relationships? Do you prioritize time in God's Word? Do you prioritize rest and worship? Do you prioritize delighting in the Lord? Do you prioritize serving others? Do you prioritize the Kingdom of God?

When adding things to your calendar, start asking yourself, Am I keeping it simple here? Will this time spent be worth it?

2. Everything we spend

Money is such an interesting thing in our culture. I think Richard Foster sums it up perfectly with this quote: "The modern hero is the poor boy who becomes rich, rather that the rich boy who purposefully becomes poor. We call being covetous ambition."[4] Wow.

Keeping it simple is a habit many Western Christians struggle with because it directly opposes our affluent lifestyle. We buy things like new cars or bigger houses to impress people we don't know instead of buying things that genuinely will make our lives better. Ironically, we buy things we don't need hoping to find fulfillment through them instead of using that same money to be generous to others, which would give us far more fulfillment than the thing we will eventually throw away.

Keeping it simple allows us to have money instead of money having us. Here are a few things to ask yourself regularly that will help you keep it simple:

- Have I already tithed and given the Lord what is His?
- Am I buying this to make my life better or to be impressive?
- Can I actually afford this?
- Do I really need the newest version of this?
- Would this purchase be good stewardship of what God has given me?
- Is there something that I could do with this money that makes more sense?
- Do I need it now?
- Is there something I could give away?

3. Everything we pursue

We've already talked about the resource of time and how valuable it is. But it's not just what we do that matters eternally, it's what we think about. What dreams do you find yourself thinking about over and over again? What goals do you have for yourself and your family? Everyone has goals. Whether they've ever been written down or said out loud doesn't matter. We are all pursuing something. What is it that you are pursuing with your life? Is it worth chasing?

I know a man who spent time in prayer every day for fifty years. He would daily ask God to show him which dreams he needed to drop and which ones he needed to pick up. He told me when he started that daily prayer, his dreams looked much different from what they look like now. Fifty years ago he had hopes for a big piece of property with a massive ranch house. He was hoping to retire early and take his dream car to car shows with his friends. He had even picked out a little beach house he'd hoped to afford, so he and his wife could play golf half of the year while most of the country was freezing during the winter months.

After half a century of praying, his dreams are totally different. God did give him the piece of property, but he has no desire to retire. God also gave him a ranch house with lots of room for guests. He and his wife have dedicated themselves to the ministry of marriage and pour into people throughout the year in their home. They give away over half of what they make and are filled with immense joy. Notice how many of his dreams did come true when he held them with an open hand and sought the Kingdom of God first! He kept it simple, and it led to being satisfied.

So ask yourself: Will my dream matter in fifty years? Will it help others or just me? Do I like where I'm headed? With each decision, ask yourself: Will this help me or hurt me in seeing Jesus?

You can do this. Keep it simple.

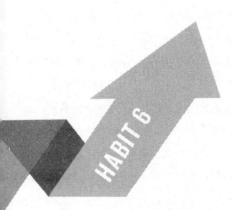

Find a Coach

REGGIE WAYNE PLAYED FOOTBALL for the Indianapolis Colts for fourteen incredible seasons. Wayne played wide receiver, and currently ranks top ten all-time in catches and received yards. The man who once wore number 87 for the Colts will likely end up in the Football Hall of Fame one day very soon.

I remember watching Reggie Wayne as a kid. He was so smooth. Smooth is what you call a football player who is incredibly good but never looks like he is trying too hard. I would watch as a defender would stay close to Reggie as he ran down the field, until the very last second when Reggie would make a quick hesitation move and then blow by the person assigned to defend him. They didn't stand a chance. He was fast, he was smart, and he had the trust of his teammates.

Reggie Wayne was clearly an NFL star. But what made him so good? By NFL standards, he definitely was not the biggest guy. He was fast by my standards, but compared to the other NFL wide receivers, he was just average. He couldn't jump the highest. He didn't have bigger hands to help him catch better. What was his *edge*?

If you aren't super into football, let me explain the preseason. Every year, a month or two before the actual season starts, players from every NFL team show up for practice, drills, scrimmages, and exhibition games against other teams in the NFL that don't count on your official record.

The preseason culture for the NFL's best players is this: Practice very little, play very little, and be around very little. The best players don't have much to improve on. They also don't do much during the preseason because they don't want to risk getting injured before the season even starts. Because of all of these factors and more, it is very normal for the good players to be seen in street clothes on the sidelines, hanging out while the young or inexperienced players are practicing and competing. This was not the case for Reggie Wayne.

From day one, Reggie Wayne never missed a practice. He was the first one there and the last one to leave. His insane work ethic stayed the same, even when he became one of the best receivers in the entire National Football League. Wayne was obsessive over his craft. He wanted every detail of his game to be scrutinized, looked over, and coached.

Every preseason, Reggie became known for wanting to be coached like a rookie. In other words, he didn't want to be treated like the future Hall of Fame wide receiver that he was, but as someone who had accomplished nothing yet. He wanted to be pushed. He desired to get better more than he wanted the comfort of the sidelines.

Reggie Wayne wanted a coach, and it changed his entire career. If you'll find the right coach, it could change your entire life, too. The closest thing we have to coaching in the Christian life is called discipleship. I've found, particularly in the next generation of Jesus followers, the word *discipleship* doesn't exactly bring about warm and fuzzy feelings. Most hear the word *discipleship* and either don't fully understand why it's so important or picture a completely inaccurate representation of what true discipleship looks like.

This negative view of discipleship is often not the case outside the church. While business leaders and marketplace gurus might not call it discipleship, it is very clear they see the need to learn from someone further along.

A good coach can change a game. A great coach can change a life.
legendary basketball coach John Wooden

Your mentors in life are important, so choose them wisely.
bestselling author and financial guru Robert Kiyosaki

If I have seen further, it is simply by standing on the shoulders of giants.
revolutionary scientist Isaac Newton

Whose shoulders are you standing on? Perhaps the most popular example in the Bible of discipleship (outside of the twelve disciples and Jesus) is between Paul and Timothy. We will go more in depth in the next chapter on how to find a Timothy to coach/disciple. We'll start here by looking at Paul's journey. Before he could get to the point of helping others, he needed help himself. That help came from a person named Barnabas.

After Paul had his famous conversion—from killing Christians to becoming one—he needed a next step. That next step, in large part, was a relationship with Barnabas. Barnabas had a great reputation. He actually helped start the early church and had built up credibility with its leaders. He was a faithful and fruitful man of God who was not intimidated by Paul's past, but instead was excited about what his future could look like.

Paul traveled all over Asia Minor with Barnabas. Their travels spanned several years as they started dozens of churches together, taught the Word of God together, and did just about everything side by side. There was no area in each of their lives that was hidden from the other. Paul was being coached. Better yet, Paul was being discipled, and it was one of the reasons he went on to become a dynamic force for the Kingdom of God.

So what is discipleship? Let's first talk about what discipleship is not. Discipleship is not the same things as mentorship. You can be mentored without ever being discipled. The key difference is that discipleship adds a spiritual component. It's everything that may come with mentorship, but it includes an intentional pursuit of Jesus together. If you are becoming a better person—a better man, a better woman, a better employee, a better dad, a better mom, etc.—but not a better follower of Christ, you are being mentored and not discipled.

Someone who is truly discipling you will not say "I think" more than "the Bible says." Authentic discipleship is always rooted first and foremost in the authority of Scripture. My favorite definition of a disciple comes from author and scholar Dallas Willard. He called himself "an apprentice of Jesus." That's what we should all desire to be, first and foremost.

A famous use of the word *apprentice* in our modern culture comes from the heroic tales of *Star Wars*. Luke Skywalker was an apprentice in the ways of the Force and the Jedi. He learned how to become a Jedi by receiving his training from Obi-Wan Kenobi and master Yoda.

As Christians, we should first and foremost be apprentices of Jesus Christ. But we can grow in our relationship with Jesus exponentially when we allow coaching and personal discipleship from those who are further along in their journey with Christ.

Discipleship was, after all, the strategy of Jesus. He spent every day teaching, correcting, coaching, mentoring, praying for, and leading a group of twelve young men as they followed Him. Those twelve disciples are the reason that you and I know about Christ today. They took what they saw and learned and, in the power of the Holy Spirit, spread it around the world with such effectiveness that now, over two thousand years later, we are still talking about and learning from them. This is the power of discipleship!

And yet, discipleship has lost its appeal to many. Discipleship isn't fast growth. It's not sexy. It's hard work that requires time, intentional sacrifice, and getting deeply involved with imperfect people. And as we all know, that can get messy fast. Because of the difficulty of discipleship, its lack of immediate results, and many other factors, we've seen believers abandon their desire to be discipled altogether. In fact, we've even seen church leaders abandon discipleship methods.

It is much more popular in today's church to hear talks on the importance of leadership than it is to hear about the importance of discipleship. Leadership doesn't require the same messy, deep work of discipleship. Leadership is much easier to be good at without the need for others to see the real, flawed version of ourselves.

Leadership podcasts are all over the internet. We have dedicated teams at church whose sole focus is to "develop leaders." We call the highest form of serving at the local church level our "leadership team." Meanwhile, discipleship's popularity seems to get smaller and smaller.

It makes sense why so many leaders find themselves burned out, struggling, or even morally failing. We have many leaders who have never been discipled. We need both. But the primary need is for discipleship.

My good friend and brilliant leader Grant Skeldon said this about the next generation leaving the church: "The church doesn't have a millenial problem. It has a discipleship problem."[1] He's right. Discipleship solves many of our current spiritual problems.

Someone who is being discipled has someone to turn to with spiritual problems and doesn't need to try to find the answer on the internet. Someone being discipled is talked out of making selfish and foolish decisions before it's too late. Someone being discipled doesn't give up on church after being hurt by someone, because there is someone to help make clear the difference between hurt caused by the church and hurt caused by people. Someone who is actively discipled feels less lonely. Someone who is actively discipled learns to read the Word and hide its truth in his or her heart. People who are discipled look less and less like a dying world and more and more like a living Christ—they are hosts of the Holy Spirit!

Discipleship is messy, slow, and not always quantifiable. But discipleship was the church growth strategy of Jesus, and it is still by far the most effective one. We all need to be discipled.

I have many friends who are not being discipled because they have the wrong perception of what they should be looking for in a coach. They think they have to find someone who is good at everything they want to be good at in order for effective discipleship to take place. Many young people think they can only learn something from famous Christian influencers or their favorite celebrity pastor. All of this is false.

The best people to disciple you will fit these criteria:

1. They are local.
2. They are further along than you are spiritually.
3. They do at least one thing you want to do.
4. They are willing to disciple you.

Discipleship is messy, slow, and not always quantifiable. But discipleship was the church growth strategy of Jesus, and it is still by far the most effective one.

If they fit those four things, your discipleship will be better than you can imagine. Let's dive into each of these a little bit more.

1. They are local

It is easier to have a mentorship relationship over the internet than it is to have a discipleship relationship. Discipleship is "follow me as I follow Christ," and it's hard to truly follow someone who you only see when the camera is on. You need access to his or her life in a way that the internet simply cannot provide.

Look for someone who can include you in parts of his or her regular schedule. Someone you can have breakfast with, go for a walk with, call at the last minute to talk, run errands with, and have access to that doesn't require a scheduled Zoom call. When it comes to discipleship, living near each other should be a priority.

2. They are further along than you are spiritually

Someone who is at the same level as you spiritually can offer great friendship, great companionship, and maybe even great advice from time to time, but not great discipleship. That person cannot give you greater intimacy with Jesus because it is not something he or she currently has.

You need someone who looks like Jesus in a way that you want for your own life. Your eyes should not be set on famous people, but fruitful people. People who have years of faithfulness to others, to their families, and in their own personal relationship with the Lord. You need a Yoda, not another apprentice.

3. They do at least one thing you want to do

You don't need someone who does *everything* you want to do in life, just one thing that matters deeply to you. If you believe God is calling you to be a great business leader, public speaker, volunteer worship leader, and writer, the chances of you finding someone who is also called to each of those things—in the exact way you are—are slim to none. Instead, find someone who meets the other criteria for discipleship and who is good at one or two of the things you hope to be good at.

Maybe you haven't found a writer or worship leader, but someone immensely talented at running a business and treating people the way Jesus would treat people. You can be discipled by multiple people and learn different things from each of them. Don't waste time trying to find the perfect mentor, find a great one and start taking notes.

4. They are willing to disciple you

A good person to disciple you needs to have the time and desire to actually prioritize your discipleship, or it will never work. The good news is this: The best followers of Jesus understand that their legacy is not *what* they will leave behind but *who*.

A sign of spiritual maturity is the desire to disciple. You would be shocked at how many are praying someone like you would take them to coffee and ask. So go ask! Even if they say no, it will be taken as a great compliment.

HABIT: FIND A GOOD COACH AND BE SPECIFIC ABOUT YOUR EXPECTATIONS

Step 1: Ask. Find a coach who fits the criteria mentioned. Take him or her to coffee, breakfast, or lunch, and offer to pay. Be clear and intentional about what you are asking.

"I look up to you more than you know. Not just what you do but how you do it. I think I could really learn a lot from you about life in general, but even more than that, I think I could learn a lot from you spiritually. Would you consider discipling me over the next year?"

Step 2: Clarify. Once you've found someone who has agreed to disciple you, set up a framework for the discipleship. This step is hugely important. The goal is to find someone to disciple you who knows exactly what you are desiring, and has that same desire to give back to you. Clarity is important!

When and how often will you regularly meet? How can you work together to make sure that the relationship is discipleship and not mentorship? In what areas of their life can you regularly be included? Is there a portion of the Bible you can walk through together? What are some areas of life that you need to work on submitting to the Lord? What are some areas you need accountability with?

Step 3: Be Prepared. Actively learn and be respectful of their time. If you don't have a small notebook, buy one. Bring the notebook and a pen with you every time you get together. Come prepared with thought-out questions. They can be family questions, Bible questions, financial questions, or just general life questions. Never show up to meet with the person discipling you without questions to ask them.

A good mentor is going to have questions for you because he or she cares about you, but don't get it twisted. The point of your time together is not for you to talk about yourself or impress them. The point of the relationship is for you to draw out and take advantage of the wealth of wisdom sitting across the table from you. You should be doing the majority of the listening.

When your questions are answered, take notes. Apply what he or she tells you. When someone sees that the time invested in you is making a difference, that person will want to invest more.

Step 4: Bless. Figure out ways you can be a blessing. Your mentor is solving a problem in your life. He or she is helping to solve the problem of a lack of spiritual intimacy. He is helping increase your biblical literacy. She is helping guide you in making good decisions. How can you help them? Is there some way you could make their life easier? You don't have to solve a massive problem for them, but when you actively look for ways to invest back, to show your gratitude by blessing them, you will always be better off for it.

Find a coach and let them coach you like a rookie. Give them access to every area of your life and the permission to say the hard things that you don't always want to hear. Discipleship can be messy. But if you'll let this habit become a part of your life, you will see the fruit of it for generations to come.

Go find a coach.

HABIT 7

Be a Coach

THE SCARIEST PLACE in the entire world for me is a home improvement store, like Home Depot.

I didn't grow up in a home where power tools existed. If something broke, we said a prayer that our neighbor knew how to fix it for us. We didn't know how to remodel a house; we knew how to talk about what we would like the house to look like. The Herrin family didn't build things, we built sermons.

Every time I step into Home Depot, I get nervous for a plethora of reasons. The first reason is because it's massive. How in the world do people find their way around such a disorienting place? Second, I don't know what 99 percent of the items in the store are even called. I pretty much stay on Google the entire time I'm there as I try to figure out what the different tools are for. And third, those nice people in orange aprons just won't leave me alone. The workers at Home Depot are *so* nice. When

I'm at Home Depot, however, I'm trying to get in and out without anyone noticing I don't know what I'm doing there.

A few years ago my wife and I bought a new house. We were so excited—finally a place of our own to call home! On move-in day we realized something was missing in our home: blinds for the windows. We had just paid for an entire new house with sixteen windows and not a single one of them had come with blinds installed. Talk about the ultimate "batteries not included" situation.

I will never forget my wife, Maddy, looking over at me in the doorway of our new home and asking me the dreaded question: "Will you go to Home Depot?"

I had no choice. I couldn't let my wife know I was scared. I couldn't let her know that her question literally sent a shiver down my spine. No. I had to look her squarely in the eyes and tell her it was no problem and that I'd be right back with blinds.

A few minutes later I pulled up to Home Depot with a song blaring through my speakers about God beckoning me to the vast unknown. . . . When I got inside the store that day, I set out on a mission to find blinds as fast as I could. Thirty-seven minutes later, I finally found the aisle with blinds. Only my worst fears were realized when I saw a Home Depot employee in that bright orange apron standing right in front of me.

"Hi! Do you need any help?" the young-looking employee asked. I have never needed more help in my entire life.

"Nope. I'm good!" I replied.

After I spent about ten minutes staring intently at different blinds without ever picking any off the shelf, the employee came back to me and asked if I was sure I didn't need help. The second time, I obliged. I opened up to this stranger about my fears of not knowing what I was doing, how his bright orange apron scared me more than I cared to admit, and that I had never put up blinds in my life.

The employee kindly talked me down from the ledge. He helped me pick out all the right sizes, and even walked with me to the front of the store to pay. When I was just about to walk out, he looked at me and tried to encourage me with these words: "Listen, man, you've got this. We have grandmas who come in here all the time who put up their own blinds. If they can do it, you definitely can. You've got this."

About five hours later, our house looked like a war zone. Boxes of blinds were lying scattered all around our home, my small tool kit had been completely emptied, and not one single pair of blinds had been installed. In the process of trying to figure out how to install the blinds, a screw had fallen from the window and cut the side of my face. I was literally putting blood, sweat, and tears into these blinds. All I could think about were the Home Depot employee's words: "We have grandmas who come in here all the time who put up their own blinds." I needed one of those grandmas.

My wife, who is by far my biggest encourager and supporter, couldn't help but laugh as she watched me struggling to figure it all out. As I was wrestling with screws and tiny plastic pieces, pretty much guessing how to make sense of the contraption in my hand, Maddy quietly sat down and opened up the small paper instruction booklet found in each box of blinds. After a few minutes she stood up, grabbed my drill from me, and easily put up the first pair. Then she looked at me, smiled, and said, "I'll take it from here, Bob the Builder."

I think a lot of times, as followers of Jesus, we make things scarier and more confusing than they have to be. *How exactly do I obey Jesus in the crazy world I live in? What if I miss what God is calling me to do? What should I be doing with my life, anyway? Am I missing something?*

Could it be that as we are stressed and anxious, hoping to find the answers to our faith questions like these, there is a clear instruction manual sitting right next to us that we are simply failing to read? Could we realize that if we simply follow what Jesus said to do, the answers to many of our questions would find us faster than we could find them?

If you feel like something is missing in your walk with the Lord, may I suggest that maybe you don't need a new word from God, but to go back and obey the last one He gave?

Therefore go and make disciples of all nations, baptizing them in the name of the Father and of the Son and of the Holy Spirit, and teaching them to obey everything I have commanded you. And surely I am with you always, to the very end of the age.

Matthew 28:19–20

Jesus' last words should be our first priority. Are we actively making disciples? The final message of Jesus was to go and to make disciples. He didn't say go make leaders or social media followers. He didn't say go write good sermons or beautiful worship songs. He urged us to focus on making disciples.

It is no shocker to me that many of the Christians I talk to who feel like they do not know their calling have never actually made a disciple. We cannot share in God's purpose when we do not also share in God's priorities. The most effective way to reach a lost world for Jesus is to make disciples. It just so happens that the most effective way to feel like you are being used by God is also to make disciples.

Jesus discipled the twelve. The twelve discipled the early Church. Barnabas was a part of the early Church. Barnabas discipled Paul. Paul discipled church leaders all over the world and happened to write a large portion of the Bible. Those church leaders and that Bible have led directly to the discipleship of millions and millions of people around the world. Including you.

So who are you discipling? Making disciples is not something that is just the pastor's job. It's not something just for people who are in full-time ministry. Discipleship is not something for people who have been following Jesus for a certain amount of time. Making disciples was a command of Jesus for *everybody* who calls Him Lord. After receiving coaching for yourself, the next step in being an apprentice of Jesus is to begin coaching others.

The most effective way to reach a lost world for Jesus is to make disciples. It just so happens that the most effective way to feel like you are being used by God is also to make disciples.

A few years back, I was leading a college ministry. It was a blast. Within the first year or so, we had grown exponentially. Every Thursday night we were having powerful services where the presence of God was tangible and lives were being changed. Word began to spread—around our small town, and eventually around the country—about what was happening. Almost every week people from other states were showing up to see what was happening. It felt different and special.

Until one day it didn't. One day the growth of the ministry suddenly came to a grinding halt. We weren't going backward, but we weren't adding dozens of new people every week either. It felt more and more difficult to keep leaders on the team. I was exhausted from feeling like I had to constantly motivate others to be as excited and expectant as I was every week. I was physically tired from spending all of my free time trying to meet new people that I could invite myself.

I started seeking the Lord about some of my frustrations. *God, what am I doing wrong? This doesn't feel sustainable. Why am I so tired? Why does this thing feel like it is suddenly going the wrong way?*

A few weeks later, I was in the mountains of Colorado on a retreat, being poured into by other leaders. One morning I was sitting outside talking with God when my soul heard a word that would change every part of my life.

You have an impressive ministry that looks nothing like me.

Whoa. I remember feeling like the thought came out of nowhere. But then I couldn't shake it. I knew it was from

God. *Okay, God . . . tell me more*, I remember thinking. *What does that even mean? It would be nice if You could drop a few more clarifying thoughts, Lord. It kind of feels like You just dropped part of what You wanted to say, and not the rest.*

For the next few weeks, I could not stop thinking about the word the Lord gave me. I started looking at everything under a microscope—what we were doing as a ministry and everything I was doing as an individual—and comparing it to God's Word. As I did, some things became abundantly clear to me.

We were an impressive ministry. We had grown from nothing to hundreds of college students within a year's time. Our podcast was averaging over ten thousand weekly downloads from young people around the country. Pastors from churches twelve hours away were driving to see one of our services in hopes that they could take some of what we had back with them. When ministry leaders showed up, they were blown away that we could get college students to consistently attend church at all. Yes, we were impressive. But we didn't look like Jesus.

We had the best worship out there. We created environments people wanted to be in. We had passion through the roof. The talks that we gave were intentional and thoughtful. But we were not making disciples; we were making consumers.

It was impressive, but it was not like Jesus. Exciting, but not going to last. Genuinely helpful, but not effective for the long term. A great strategy for ministry growth, but not the best strategy to grow heaven. We were doing things that sounded good to us that Jesus never emphasized. We were not making disciples.

So I did what anyone would do in that situation. I started asking God who I should disciple. I remember being like, *You are right, God. We will change things up. Where should I start? Send me someone to disciple, and I'll do my best to model it before I start asking others to do it.*

Around the time I started those prayers, I noticed a new college freshman showing up to our ministry. The guy was outgoing and seemed very social. He looked athletic and seemed to always have girls nearby. Just from watching him from afar, I could tell he was a little immature and girl-crazy. He was also slightly obnoxious, and it felt like he would often come up to talk to me just so other people would see him around me. Particularly whatever Christian girl he was trying to impress that week.

After a while, he started asking me if we could get coffee sometime. I wanted no part of that. He didn't seem like the kind of guy I would like to hang out with. Every time he would ask, I would either be busy or find a reason to be busy so I didn't have to go.

One Thursday night, before our service started, I was in my office praying specifically for someone to disciple. When I finished praying, I went outside of the building. Hundreds of college students were already there, thirty minutes early, hanging out, playing cornhole, and listening to the music our DJ was playing. As I stood looking around, my eyes locked on the obnoxious freshman guy.

That's the guy.

Once the thought came into my mind, I couldn't shake it. *Really, God? That guy? Seriously?* The next day we got coffee. At the end of what was a wild forty-five-minute conversation, I jumped right into it. "Hey, man. Listen. I'm really glad you've been coming to our ministry. I hope you are getting something out of it. I know that you've been wanting to become better friends, but I really feel like God is asking me to start making disciples. So I have an offer for you. We can become much better friends, but it's going to cost you. I'm going to start including you in every part of my life. From my quiet time to my sermon prepping to my grocery shopping. I'm going to pour into your life in the best way I know how for the next year. But in return, I'm going to ask you to take it seriously."

He quickly accepted. I had no idea that day that I was talking to a guy who would one day become like a little brother to me. I also had no idea how dramatically our ministry would change. How we would go from being impressive to powerful. From large to effective. From consumers to disciples.

We met every Monday morning at a coffee shop and read and discussed Scripture together. He was at my house constantly. I invited him to meetings with me, took him on ministry trips, and stayed up late talking him out of relationship after relationship. We prayed together. I started asking for more from him at our ministry events. He went from being the ministry flirt to being one of our core leaders. When we launched small groups, he oversaw the entire ministry.

About a year into our relationship, I walked into our regular coffee shop one afternoon and noticed him sitting on the other side of the room with what looked like another young college guy. They both had their Bibles out and were talking very intently. I didn't want to bother them, so I grabbed a coffee and sat on the other side of the room. About thirty minutes later, their meeting ended, and my friend came over to me.

"What were you guys doing over there, bro?" I asked.

"Oh—that guy? I started discipling him a couple months ago. He's going to be a good one."

HABIT: BE A COACH

There are a lot of great discipleship frameworks out there. Yours will and probably should be different from mine. But the first step is always the same: Identify the right person to pour into.

Here are a few things you should look for to find the right candidate:

1. Someone who is a little behind you spiritually.
   - You can't give what you don't have.
   - Discipleship is not the same thing as an accountability partner. You should clearly be the person who is spiritually further along.
2. Someone who is the same sex.
   - If you are married, this should be self-explanatory. Discipleship requires a closeness that isn't appropriate for you to have with someone of the opposite sex.

- If you are single, don't try to disciple someone from the opposite sex either. Discipleship is a deep relationship. The intention of discipleship is great intimacy with Jesus, not unintentional intimacy with each other.

3. Someone who is good soil.
   - Look for someone who either already has fruit or someone who is ready to start growing. The guy I started to disciple at our college ministry didn't have much fruit at the time, but he was ready. He was excited and clearly ready to grow if someone took the time to invest in him.

4. Someone who is hungry.
   - You want to disciple someone who is self-motivated. They have to want to be discipled just as much as you want to disciple them.

5. Someone who does what they say they are going to do.
   - If they are not dependable, the discipleship will probably never happen. Make sure they (and you) are someone who will show up when they say they will.

One you've identified who you are going to coach (disciple), it's time to start the habit. As you will find, it is extremely hard to create time to disciple someone. So you shouldn't. At least, not always. What I mean is this: You don't have to clear your schedule for them, just include them in the schedule you already have.

If you go running on Monday mornings, invite them to run with you. If you lead a Bible study on Tuesday nights at your church, ask them to start going with you. If you have kids to take to school, invite them to ride with you. Discipleship is not a personal small group meeting. It's doing life intentionally with someone else, letting them follow you as you follow Jesus in every area of your life.

Here are the three main areas where you should try to invite those you disciple:

1. Include them in your time with the Lord
2. Include them in your time with family
3. Include them in your fun time

This allows them to grow as a Jesus follower in every area of their life. Observing your life shows them how to apply the Bible, not just memorize it. Remember, the goal is to make disciples who live the Word, not just know it.

As you begin to disciple others, you will realize that it is not just mandatory for followers of Jesus, it's beneficial. The person you are discipling will grow closer to Jesus. The things you do will get better because they are watching.

No one learns as much about a subject as one who is forced to teach it.

Peter Drucker

As you disciple others, you will grow even more in Christ yourself.

Start coaching!

Sit in Silence

IN 2013, I WAS TRYING to figure out college life. I was a freshman at Lee University in Cleveland, Tennessee, and I was having a blast. I went to most of my classes, my friend circle was growing daily, and I was eating way too much fast food.

In 2013, many things were different from what they are now. The fashion was different. The way we used social media was much different. Even the music was different. One day after class, my roommate Tyler picked me up to give me a ride back to our dorm. I hopped into his Ford Explorer, and we took off down the road. Tyler turned up the volume on his car stereo and asked me, "Have you heard of this new band? They're called Twenty One Pilots."

Today, Twenty One Pilots is one of the most famous bands in the United States. In 2013 I hadn't heard of them, but I already knew I liked them. The melody was unique. The singer was kind of singing and rapping at the same time. It was cool. But as I listened to the song titled "Car Radio," the lyrics stood out the most.

The lead singer, Tyler Joseph, is telling about having his car radio stolen, and now when he gets in the car, he has to sit in silence. And the silence is deafening. He realizes that the noise helped distract him from the things that were real that he didn't want to address. He has to go without noise, and he doesn't like it one bit. His words are profound.

It's been almost a decade since I heard "Car Radio" for the first time. Then, I thought the lyrics were cool and interesting. Now when I listen, I think they directly address one of the great spiritual problems of our day: We don't know how to be silent.

Silence will always be unwelcome when we are afraid of addressing what is beneath the surface of our souls. But a Christian life should be one that drags what is beneath the surface into the light, so that Jesus can address what we would not address otherwise.

Jesus does not wish to serve as a Band-Aid for the problems you feel comfortable posting about on social media. Jesus came for those problems too, yes. But Jesus wants to go beneath the surface. The healing that Jesus offers is soul deep. He is less like a Band-Aid and much more like a surgeon, carefully and compassionately working on your innermost self, never intimidated by the messiness of the job.

We need to be quiet on purpose, so that we can meet with the healer of our souls. Richard Foster famously said that our enemy, the devil, majors in three things: noise, hurry, and crowds. Foster believes that through these three things, the devil can keep us distracted and too busy for God to do the work He wants to do in our souls.[1]

You know as well as I do that distractions are everywhere. We see this in the frantic and hurried way that our culture lives. We fly through life like busy little ants. When we finish one task, it is immediately time to move to the next one. Our to-do lists seem endless. Even when our day is finished, our mind is not. The continual next thing takes up the exact mental real estate that God so desperately desires to occupy inside of us. C. G. Jung is quoted as saying something that resonates with me: "Hurry is not of the devil. It is the devil."

The way we fly through life, one thing after the next, is killing us spiritually. Our obsession with moving quickly allows us to do more, but it is causing us to be less. While our heart and soul long for God, we are running right past Him. N. T. Wright put it beautifully when he said, "If we were prepared to slow down a bit . . . we might actually be able . . . to catch [up to] God."[2]

What we need is a speed bump. We need something to slow us down long enough to see and hear. We need something that helps eliminate distractions. We need to learn to sit in silence.

If you are using distraction and noise to keep yourself from addressing sin, anxiety, and insecurity, then a time of silence can feel like turmoil, as you are forced to think about and even deal with those issues. But to someone who believes the best thing that can happen to them is for Jesus to have *all* of their life, silence can serve as a beautiful kind of turmoil. Silence can be an uprising against your flesh and all the things that are holding you back from a deeper and more intimate relationship with your Savior.

Silence can turn into something you desire, instead of being something you fear. The ability to enjoy silence with another, after all, is an indicator of a healthy relationship. The need for noise in a relationship is often a sign of it being surface level. Rich Villodas puts the idea this way: "Our ability to be silent with someone is largely contingent on our level of intimacy or familiarity with that person."[3]

If you have a new friend and you are sitting at a coffee shop together, being silent can get awkward really fast. When the conversation stops, uncomfortableness begins quite quickly. There is an unspoken desire from both people to say something right away to keep the conversation going. In new relationships, noise is comforting and connecting. But in deep relationships, silence is seen as intimacy.

My wife and I sit together in silence at coffee shops all the time. We talk at them, too, to be sure. But many times we sit still, enjoying each other's presence without the need for words. The lack of talking is not a worry for us. We are not wondering what the other person thinks about us during those moments—because we know. We are able to be silent and enjoy it because our relationship is so intimate that we've graduated beyond the need for noise.

Jesus wants you to graduate beyond the need for noise. The only way for you to graduate beyond the need for noise is for you to fall in love with what happens in silence. Jesus loved silence. In fact, right in the thick of Jesus' ministry in the gospels, He developed the habit of getting away to what the Bible calls "lonely places" (Luke 5:16). When Jesus heard that John the Baptist had been beheaded, He withdrew to a solitary place (see Matthew 14:13). The quiet place became where Jesus went as a sanctuary to pray before big decisions (see Luke 6:12). He prayed alone on a mountaintop after performing miracles (see Matthew 14:20–23).

I've found that you learn to be silent by being silent. The more you do it, the more you love it. The more time you spend in silence, the more you see its fruit in your life. Our silence helps us stay present with God. When our attention is on God, we don't want to pay attention to anything else because we realize that there is nothing else worth paying attention to more.

If we claim to be followers of Jesus, perhaps we should try following Him to the quiet place. I tried it, and it quite literally changed my life. When Covid-19 first shut down the world in the spring of 2020, I remember everyone thinking it would be a short-term problem. I think our initial assumption was that we would all stay inside for a week or two while the scientists did some research and eventually told us that we were all going to be fine. Then we would all be allowed to go back to normal life. Boy were those assumptions wrong.

About a month into the pandemic, silence and stillness were violently attacking my soul. My to-do list couldn't distract me anymore because for the first time in my life, I had finished everything on it! We weren't allowed to go places, be with people, or even go to work regularly. There

You learn to be silent by being silent. The more you do it, the more you love it. The more time you spend in silence, the more you see its fruit in your life. Our silence helps us stay present with God.

was a lot of solitude, a lot of silence, and a lot of being alone with my own thoughts. I hated it.

As I began to realize that maybe my soul wasn't as healthy as I thought it was, I started seeking the Lord, wanting to know why I was so discontent and unhappy. Obviously, there was a lot going on in the world that was troubling and sad, but what I was feeling was more than those things. It felt like without working for God or speaking for God, I wasn't really hearing or feeling God.

Enter the habit of sitting in silence. I had heard John Mark Comer talk about how he regularly sits in silence as part of his time with the Lord each morning. It sounded strange to me. Honestly, it sounded like a waste of time. If I was going to just sit in silence, I might as well pray, right? At least that way I was making the most of that time. Prayer seemed like a much better investment of my time. But then something crazy happened. I tried sitting in silence.

It wasn't great at first. My mind was so used to being distracted that after just a few moments of sitting quietly in our living room, I was thinking about what I wanted to go make for breakfast. But even on that first day, I felt something different in my soul. For the first time in a long time, I felt like I wasn't just talking to God—I was attempting to enjoy God's presence, too.

Before that day, my time with the Lord had looked very similar to this:

- Read my Bible
- Write down some thoughts and notes
- Pray

Every day since, I've ended my morning time with the Lord in a time of silence. That time has evolved, and I will share more about that when we get into the logistics of the habit, but silence has become something that I crave deeply now.

Silence takes my prayer life from a megaphone to a telephone. It gives God the space to speak back to me. It gives me the space to enjoy God's presence. It helps me fight my fleshly desire to keep my spiritual life at surface level. It drags the dark areas of my soul back into the light with Jesus. It gives me a daily opportunity to recenter, refocus, and refresh. Sitting in silence has become a deep inhale and exhale for my soul at the beginning of every day that opens the door for Jesus to take control. Sitting in silence is a game-changing habit for any who are looking for more intimacy with Jesus.

HABIT: SITTING IN SILENCE

Sitting in silence with the Lord can be done at any time, at any place. I've found that randomness can be beautiful, but it is a pretty negative ingredient for a habit. While you can practice this habit randomly, it is much better to implement it purposefully if you want it to truly take effect.

My advice would be to add it to your morning time with God. This will help it become something you remember to do daily. Again, you will not get good at sitting in silence until you actually start sitting in silence. Let's jump in to what that looks like.

When: Start by practicing this habit at the end of your morning time with the Lord. But over time, feel free to add it throughout your day as well. You can choose to sit in silence instead of listening to a podcast on your way to work in the morning. You can choose to sit in silence in your office for a few minutes after a Zoom meeting. You can choose to practice this habit in a plethora of places, and it will always be beneficial to your soul.

The goal: Silence by itself has no power. Silence without listening to God or enjoying God's presence is actually pointless. When we practice the habit of silence, we have to intentionally start with the goal of meeting with God. Our goal is to focus our emotions, attentions, and thoughts on the Spirit of God as we are silent.

My secret sauce: Over the last couple years of practicing this habit, I've changed how I do it quite a bit. I still practice it every morning after my Bible time, but instead of practicing it at our kitchen table or in my room, I now go outside. This habit is the *best* outside.

If you have somewhere close that you can walk to while practicing being silent with the Lord, I highly recommend doing it. There is something about a silent walk with the Lord while taking in His creation that opens up our minds and our souls to commune with God in a way that is truly revelatory. Don't take your phone with you, or even worship music. Just take your body outside and walk. Let your soul breathe. Let your mind relax. Let God speak to you.

I do this every morning. Sometimes for ten minutes. Sometimes as long as thirty minutes. There are some mornings when sitting in silence feels more like a nature walk than a God walk. On those mornings, I don't always hear a word from the Lord or even sense that God is with me, but that does not change the fact that He is there. Other mornings, I tangibly feel the presence of God the entire time I'm walking. He speaks to certain situations directly sometimes. There have been moments when I've been on my walk and God has brought a friend or family member into my mind that I haven't talked to in a while, and I've taken it as a sign to reach out to them. There was a morning not too long ago when our family was in the middle of making a big decision. I went for my morning walk with the Lord, and as soon as I walked back inside and checked my phone, I received a text from someone encouraging me in the exact way I needed, to make the decision I knew we were supposed to make.

God speaks when we listen. I find it easiest to listen to Him when I'm silent, surrounded by His creation with no distractions. Don't become discouraged if you attempt this habit and find it boring at first. Give it time. Don't worry if you attempt this habit and find yourself distracted. My mind often wanders to things that are not all that spiritual. In the beginning of practicing this habit, I would beat myself up for not being able to focus on the Lord. Not anymore. Every distraction is an opportunity for me to return my mind to the Lord. God loves when we return.

It's also okay to not have full focus every time we practice this habit. I believe God understands us. After all, He created us. Even if you get "nothing" out of this time on a particular day, you are getting something—you're getting used to putting yourself before the Lord. You are getting used to not having distractions or noise all the time. You are getting used to prioritizing time with the Lord. God is going to bless that.

God has done some of the most incredible things in my life on my little quiet walks with Him. Sitting in silence has allowed God to do messy, soul-level work inside of me. I crave that time with Him so much that even as I am concluding the final words of this chapter, I am already thinking about tomorrow morning's scheduled meeting with Jesus. I can't wait to sit in the silence with the Lord.

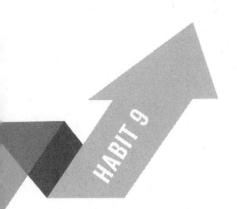

Contribute to a Team

WHEN I WAS GROWING UP, I loved to play basketball. In fact, basketball consumed most of my free time as a high schooler. I would get to school an hour early in the mornings to lift weights, stay after school for two or three hours for practice, and stay up late at night watching NBA games on TV. I loved to "hoop."

My high school basketball team was pretty good. In fact, my junior year we won the state championship in Florida for our division. It was a memory I will never forget. In part because of a guy I'll call Ben.

Ben was a really good guy. He was always kind to everyone and worked hard on the basketball court. He was about six-foot-six, had a long, wiry frame, and kind of hopped around from place to place with a funny smile on his face.

We were weeks away from the start of the season. Our practices were really ramping up, and our coach was about to make some tough decisions. We had a large group of very talented players at our high school, but the varsity team could only have twelve players dressed out (playing) and two extra players on the bench. Everyone else would have to be relegated to the junior varsity team. Things were getting competitive, and Ben was in there giving his all with the best of them.

When the team results were posted, Ben's position was on the bench. He could've done one of two things. One, he could have quit. He wasn't going to get to play much in games, yet he would still be expected to practice just like any other team member. Actually, quitting made a lot of sense.

But Ben took option number two. Every day he worked hard in practice. He played in practice like he was actually going to get to play in the games. Ben never sulked or appeared to feel bad for himself. He showed up his normal goofy self. Ben chose the much harder option.

Toward the end of our season, something unexpected happened. Our starting power forward suffered an ankle sprain and ended up missing the rest of the regular season and much of the playoffs.

Lucky for our team, Ben was ready. He was promoted to the backup power forward, and for the next seven or eight games he came off the bench and played beautifully. He truly was a sparkplug for our team and played a *huge* part in helping us win the state championship.

When I reflect back on those high school "glory days," I always think about Ben. He stayed. It didn't always make sense, but he stayed because he believed in our team, and it ended up paying off for all of us.

I'd like to start off by saying that I am well aware that the comparison I am about to make is not a perfect comparison by any stretch of the imagination. But I believe Ben's story has many similarities to what is happening right now in the American church.

Over the last several years, it has become increasingly popular to call yourself a Christian but stop going to church. It's become equally popular to share stories of church hurt as the reason for your absence or exit. This is not surprising. After all, there have been some pretty terrible things that have happened in the Church.

First off, church hurt is real. It does happen, and it's sad—not at all a reflection of the Jesus that the Church gathers to worship. Second, over the last few years we have seen scandal after scandal in the mainstream media outlets. This has been both heartbreaking and shameful for the Church. There has been so much more that has led people to leave the church, like Covid-19, theological division, financial indiscretion, and more.

Today, we as Christians have two options, much like Ben had. We can choose to leave, or we can choose to stay.

The early disciples had a choice to make, too. When Jesus ascended into heaven, they very easily could have hung it up and settled for a different version of the Church than the one that Jesus lived and so often talked about. Instead, they chose to follow Jesus—even at the expense of their own lives. If Jesus was willing to die to establish His Church, shouldn't we at least be willing to gather together to worship Him? It is a habit that is good for our faith.

Church attendance is as vital to a disciple as a transfusion of rich, healthy blood to a sick man.

Dwight L. Moody

We can choose to quit the team, or we can choose to contribute. We need to choose contribution. There are a few reasons I'm choosing to stay in the local church, even though bad things have happened.

1. It's not about me

If you approach church as a place that exists to address your needs, you will miss the point entirely. Approaching church hoping that it will fulfill your needs will leave you more disappointed than fulfilled. Church can't fulfill your needs. Only Jesus can do that.

Church is about worshipping God. We come to church hoping that through our worship of God, we might be filled. Church is not for us, it is for God.

In a culture that tells us that everything *is* about us and our needs, this can be a tough psychological change. When we are accustomed to making decisions with our ultimate happiness in mind, it is hard to suddenly make decisions with our holiness in mind. When speaking to a crowd of young millennial and Gen-Z Christians, Tim Keller said, "You are the generation most afraid of real community because it inevitably limits freedom and choice. Get over your fear."[1]

I found that statement to be so profound. I had to read it several times. We are the generation who vocally yearns for community and actively rejects what it truly looks like. We want community that doesn't cost us anything. The problem is community that doesn't cost us anything isn't real community at all. It's selfishness. The local church is where real community is supposed to take place. And most likely, at some point, it's going to cost us something.

2. Teammates make me better, even the bad ones

When we accept Christ as Lord, we are miraculously made right with God. We are saved right then and there. But there is a process that begins that very day of becoming more and more like Christ. This process is called sanctification, and it is written about all throughout the Bible.

> Let perseverance finish its work so that you may be mature and complete, not lacking anything.
>
> James 1:4

> Being confident of this, that he who began a good work in you will carry it on to completion until the day of Christ Jesus.
>
> Philippians 1:6

One of the healthiest things for our process of becoming more like Christ is for us to *not* get our way. We deny God the opportunity to mold our hearts to look like His when we refuse to be around people or situations that are not our choosing.

I see this all the time. People will join an amazing church, only to leave the first time there is a disagreement. Or join a small group and benefit from a beautiful community, only to leave the moment someone joins the group who annoys or bothers them. I've watched people allow one bad apple to convince them that the entire apple farm is bad. This is a tragedy.

It's important for us to remember that the Church is a hospital for the broken, and we are *all* broken without the person of Jesus making us whole.

I've found that being around people who look the least like me often makes me the most like Christ. Sure, if you are a part of a church where many people have similar interests and ways of thinking, it can be a lot of fun. I am not saying to run from that. But if your first response to anyone who enters your community who thinks or looks differently is to leave, you should run from that way of thinking.

Disagreements with brothers and sisters in Christ don't have to end in the breaking off community. They can end in seeking understanding and in deeper unity. People who annoy you in your small group don't have to lead you to leaving your group. They can lead you to learning how to love people a little bit more like Jesus does. People who don't do what they say they are going to do don't have to lead you to leave. They can lead you to developing patience and endurance, like James wrote about.

3. I was made to contribute

You were made to contribute to the Church. We were all made to contribute to the Church, not to a supplement of the Church. A nonprofit is not the same thing as a church.

A small group is not the Church. A missions organization or homeless shelter is not the Church. All of those places are amazing supplements to the Church, but they are not the Church.

I believe it is totally okay to simply attend a church for a season. But we must always have the perspective of contributing, or we will quickly fall into the destructive habit of consuming. Consuming costs us very little and, therefore, leads to very little fruit. Contributing costs us much and leads to much fruit. Consuming causes us to be around the things of God without ever fully benefiting from the things of God. God doesn't want you to simply sit in a chair and consume. He desires for you to contribute.

We are repeatedly referred to in the Bible as the "body" of Christ. Some days your hand is more active than your foot, but it is no less valuable. It works the same way in the Church. Every person has a part to play, and every role is important. The quicker we believe that, the quicker God can use us for His purposes.

HABIT: CONTRIBUTE TO A TEAM

Step 1: Find a local church to join. For every story of a church being bad, there are one hundred more awesome churches. Go find one!

When you are first looking for a church, it's totally okay to hop around and find the one that makes the most sense.

Every person has a part to play, and every role is important. The quicker we believe that, the quicker God can use us for His purposes.

Here are a few things I would recommend you look for when you visit:

- How is the preaching? Does the pastor preach the Bible, or does he preach inspirational nuggets?
- How does the community feel? Does it feel like a place you want to be? Do the people feel like people you could see yourself doing life with?
- What is the church's mission? Do you believe in it?
- What is the church's philosophy on serving? Is there a place you can serve there?
- Where does the church spend money? Obviously, every church has to spend money on salaries and keeping the lights on, but what do they do with the extra? What organizations do they support? What are they doing in the city to make it better?

Step 2: Contribute. If you want to get the most out of the local church, you cannot simply be a spectator—you must grow into being a contributor. Here are a few easy ways you can contribute to what God is doing:

1. Show up consistently.

   You can't reap the benefits of the local church if you are not regularly there. Occasionally missing church for something is totally understandable, as long as it is the exception and not the norm. Show up!

2. Lean in.

As a pastor, I am always amazed by the power of a dozen people in a room who are *leaned in* to what God is doing and how it can impact everyone else. I have literally been in services where a small section of people who are taking notes, worshipping passionately, and actively engaging in the service have totally transformed the spirit of everyone else in the room. The way you participate at church, even in the small things, is contagious.

3. Be a part of community.

If the only time you interact with the people at your local church is on Sundays and on Instagram, you are doing it wrong. The point is to get to know each other and to do life together. Our relationship with God grows deeper as we experience the ups and the downs of community. A good local church community will be there for you to help carry burdens. They will harbor some of your greatest friendships, and they will sharpen you in more ways than one. A good local church community will also stretch you. They will give you opportunities to love others and respond to situations the way that Christ would. Community is necessary for your growth in Christ.

4. Serve.

We are never more like Christ than when we are serving others for the glory of God. After you've spent some time doing steps one through three, it's time to find a way to *serve*. Unfortunately, I've found that most people think the only way they can serve is to be a part of a "serve team" at their church. There is nothing wrong with serving on the parking lot team, as a greeter, or in the café. If that is where you feel God is calling you, by all means, *do it*. But there are a million other ways you can serve your church. If you don't think a serve team is the avenue where God is calling you, my advice would be to set up a meeting with your pastor or a staff member who can share more about the needs of the church. Ask what problems need to be solved at the church and then pray about them. God might be calling you to serve in a way that provides a solution to a major problem. The meeting might also spark ideas that you hadn't thought of on your own.

If we want to flourish the way God intended us to in our relationship with Him, we must be willing to also participate in relationships with others. A local church is the most incredible arena for this to take place. When we put ourselves firmly on a team and contribute to that team regularly, we set ourselves up to go deeper with the Lord than we ever thought possible.

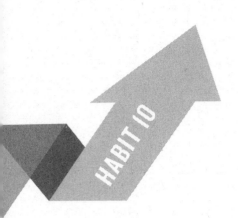

Celebrate Everything

WHEN I MET MY WIFE, MADDY, for the first time, I was absolutely convinced of two things. The first was that I had never seen a more beautiful girl in my life. The second was that I had never before met someone who always seemed to be five seconds away from her next adventure.

When I met Maddy, she was not waiting around for life to hand her anything; she was reaching out for it with both hands. At twenty-three years old, she had traveled to dozens of countries, had dinner with the actor Nicholas Cage, and had jumped out of a perfectly good airplane with a GoPro strapped to her head. The more I got to know her, the more there was to know, it seemed like. She has photos of herself with famous football players, videos of herself climbing down a mountain in the snow on New Year's Eve, and has more dance moves than she knows what to do with.

What I'm trying to say is that my wife is awesome. It wasn't just that my wife had done cool things or was a cool person that attracted me to her, though. There was something else to her. She had this quality that was magnetic. I had met a handful of other people who had a similar quality, but never anyone quite like this. I hadn't been able to put my finger on what it was until we took a trip to Nashville.

It had only been a few weeks into our relationship, but I was well aware just how far out of my league Maddy was. Because of that, I was on my absolute best behavior. We met up with a few of Maddy's friends from Nashville and headed over to the Bridgestone Arena to see the legendary Harry Styles in concert. As we were walking up to the arena, we noticed the line was literally wrapped multiple times around the building (we were clearly late to the party). Some of us groaned at the sight of the line, but not Maddy.

"Oh this will be great! We will have time to play Finish the Lyric to all the songs off Harry's new album. I'm horrible at this, but it'll be fun!" she said.

Then Maddy's friend Taylor said, "Only you could manage a way to throw confetti in a situation like this."

Throw confetti. What did that even mean? I remember not wanting to ask, fearing that maybe I was officially out of the know when it came to cool phrases people were saying in 2018. But I overcame. "What does throwing confetti mean?" I sheepishly asked.

"Well, if you haven't noticed, Noah, your girlfriend here has a habit of trying to make the most out of every situation. She calls it throwing confetti."

For the last four years of my life, I've had a front-row seat to Maddy throwing confetti. It has looked different every day. Some days it is swerving off the side of the road to pick Pampas grass from a field and make a bouquet. Other days it is taking a break from packing moving boxes to have a three-minute dance party to 2000s hits on Spotify. There was even one time when I was having a horrible day, and Maddy turned the car around and drove me to get a popsicle in downtown Birmingham.

Throwing confetti is a phrase we now use all the time in our house. It simply means to celebrate. I've learned a lot from Maddy Herrin, but one of the greatest lessons she has taught me is that throwing confetti is a crucial part of life. It's so crucial that I am convinced it's actually spiritual.

In the beginning God created the heavens and the earth, Genesis 1:1.

This is the starting verse for everything we know about life. We know that before this verse, there was God. He has always been, and He will always be. But from what we can gather, before Genesis 1:1, there wasn't much else going on besides God. Everything good that we see, smell, touch, feel, eat, and eat too much of is here because God created it. This is a pretty basic concept and probably one that you've thought about before, if you've read the Bible. I've often thought how cool it is that God was just chillin' up in heaven one day and was like, you know what this world needs? Pandas. And then poof. He created them.

God also created things we can't see or physically touch. Like our emotions. Think about this fact: According to Genesis 1:27, we were made in God's image. This means that God created emotions and feelings inside of us that are made in the image of His emotions and feelings. That is so wild to me.

My favorite feeling that God created is joy. It's so much better than sadness or craving pizza bites at two in the morning like I am while writing this. Joy is life-giving.

The Bible mentions the word *joy* four hundred and thirty different times. With that many mentions, it would seem joy is something that should be present in the life of a Christian. After all, we have so much to be joyful about because of Jesus. But for many people, joy seems to be the one thing that got away. A feeling that always seems to be just out of reach.

What happens when you know God created joy, and you know God wants you to have joy, but you just can't seem to find it? Where does one go hunting for joy? Is it even possible to grow in it?

The Bible is clear that you can in fact grow in joy. Proverbs 10:28 says, "The prospect of the righteous is joy." In other words, for believers, we have the hope of joy now but also the hope of joy in the future. We can grow in joy.

Science also supports this claim. In 2006, Harvard psychology professor Daniel Gilbert released a book titled *Stumbling on Happiness*.[1] Gilbert performed an in-depth case study on a large group of people from all different backgrounds and walks of life with the hopes of finding the truth out about one thing: Can you choose to be happier? His findings were shocking.

After studying mounds and mounds of data, Gilbert said that the majority of people were looking for big jumps toward deeper happiness. Examples included finding their dream job, marrying their dream spouse, or moving to their dream city. Gilbert's results found that these big leaps hardly ever made a person happier. In fact, people who looked for big things to solve a happiness deficit were hardly ever happier, *even the ones who successfully achieved their dreams.* Their happiness levels rose for a brief time and then went back to normal.

But there *was* a group in Daniel Gilbert's research that was exponentially growing in happiness. The most profound finding in the entire book was this simple conclusion: It was not the people who had occasionally won the "lottery of life" who are the happiest. But rather, the people who strive to find things to be happy about every single day.

Joy grows like a snowball rolling down a hill in the middle of winter. It's a fight for that thing to roll in the beginning, but every square inch it rolls down the hill is important. The snowball gains traction little by little until the momentum from the growth carries the snowball larger and farther down the hill, until you don't recognize the little snowball that started at the top.

If we practiced joy in small ways every single day, I wonder if we would even be able to recognize ourselves five years from now. What would we look like ten years? What would we feel in twenty, or thirty?

Let's check in here. So far we have two ideas in this chapter:

1. Throw confetti.
2. Small consistent decisions lead to a life with more joy.

The two points work together. The small daily decision to have joy is the "what." The confetti throwing is the "how." There is nothing that brings more joy than a good old-fashioned celebration.

Birthday parties are some of the most joyful times on the planet. There's friends, family, piñatas, and cake! But there are plenty of other examples of celebrations. In the National Football League, the Super Bowl Champions end their season with a parade through the city they represent. Every year on December 31 we celebrate everything that happened in the last three hundred and sixty-four days, and we anticipate everything that will happen in the next three hundred and sixty-four. Each of these moments, and thousands of other celebrations, are marked with the feeling of joy.

It is hard to celebrate and not feel joy. The more we feel joy, the more likely we are to become joyful. If we found something to celebrate every single day (small consistent decisions to have joy and celebrations), we would eventually be people who are naturally the most joy-filled on the planet.

1. Celebrate yourself

I believe there is a way to do this that is both helpful and honoring to the Lord. Here's what I am not saying when I say celebrate yourself: I am not saying read your own press clippings, buy your own hype, or be full of yourself. That would actually lead to you having less joy and probably having a lot fewer friends, too.

It is hard to celebrate and not feel joy. The more we feel joy, the more likely we are to become joyful. If we found something to celebrate every single day, we would eventually be people who are naturally the most joy-filled on the planet.

Celebrating yourself means celebrating things that you feel good about. Here are a few things I celebrated this week:

- I celebrated waking up at 5:30 a.m. every day to work out by buying myself some new workout shorts.
- I celebrated the Georgia Bulldogs remaining undefeated by watching the game with friends.
- I celebrated that my 15-year-old car is still giving me no issues.
- I celebrated when I cut the grass and was able to make the yard have "yard lines."
- I celebrated when I was running late for a meeting and the interstate didn't have traffic.
- I celebrated when I saw the tree in our backyard showing the first signs of fall, with dark yellow leaves.
- I celebrated when my favorite coffee shop released a new roast of coffee beans.
- I celebrated when I filled my car up at the gas station and noticed that gas prices had dropped some.
- I celebrated when my new journal came in the mail.

This week I celebrated a lot, but not many of them were big or noteworthy. Most were small, everyday things that the old Noah would have been thankful for but probably would have just moved right past. This week I didn't do that. I slowed down long enough to savor the joy and thank God. I slowed down enough to intentionally celebrate something good.

2. Celebrate others

This is where the fun really starts. Celebrating others can unlock immense joy in your life. Before we jump into celebrating others, I think we should talk a little bit about the psychology of celebrating others. There is something lurking inside of you that may resist your celebration of others. That enemy of celebrating others is called insecurity.

There is a lie that the devil speaks to us in the subconscious of our soul, and it is a sneaky one. The lie is *If I celebrate others too much, then no one will want to celebrate me.* It sounds horribly pathetic out loud, but horribly convincing in our hearts.

Another way to describe this problem is by referring to it as a "scarcity mentality." The scarcity mentality is a way of thinking that there is only so much of something, and the more that is used up, the less of it there is to go around. A scarcity mindset might have been something to worry about, oh, say a few hundred years ago when the English settlers were first learning to grow crops in America. But it is definitely not something we should worry about when celebrating others.

I've found that the people in my life who are the easiest to cheer for, congratulate, throw surprise birthday parties for, and love on are also the people who do all those things for others the best. It's almost like the more celebration you put out, the more celebration you take in. The more joy you give to other people, the more likely you are to be given joy.

This is not the only reason celebrating others should be prioritized. First Thessalonians 5:11 says, "Encourage one another and build each other up." There is nothing that can change a day for the better like the intentional and thoughtful encouragement of a true friend. Celebrating others is good for our soul, and for the souls of others.

Can I tell you a quick story? When I first started preaching, I had no idea what I was doing. Some days I still feel like I don't, but back then, I was deeply insecure about speaking in front of people. It was a real struggle for me to even stand up for thirty minutes without fainting, let alone say something that would help someone in their spiritual journey with God.

One Thursday night, I had just finished preaching, and I felt particularly bad about how it had gone. One the outside, you would have never known it. I was smiling and hanging out with people after the service like I always did. But on the inside, I just wanted to be back home, away from the embarrassment that I was feeling. In fact, I was questioning if I should even keep doing what I was doing. Surely there were people better suited than I was.

As I was walking to my car later that night, one of my best friends came running up to me. I'll never forget what he said. "Bro! I just have to say, tonight really blessed me. The words you said spoke right to where I'm at, and I deeply needed to hear that message. I also just wanted to take a second and encourage you. I know you haven't been preaching for that long, and it has got to be so nerve-racking standing up in front like that, but there is already a noticeable improvement in your preaching from just the last couple of months. I can really see that you are called to this thing, and I'm excited to watch the way God uses you."

Just like that, I went from wanting to quit preaching to wanting to preach another sermon for him right there in the parking lot! One genuine and thoughtful celebration of another person can literally change the trajectory of his or her life.

Here are a few practical examples of celebrating others:

- Texting a friend who passed a big exam they had been studying for to congratulate them.
- Buying someone a meal and thanking them for being such a great friend.
- Posting a thoughtful caption on Instagram highlighting some of the traits you admire about a person.
- Sending a box of cookies to a friend's front door when they move into a new house.
- Showing up with signs and noisemakers to cheer someone on at a competition.
- Remembering key details about things that matter to others and following up on them.

Celebrating others is probably something you already do. But if you really want to grow in joy, making a regular habit of celebrating others can expedite that journey.

3. Celebrate in bad times

First Thessalonians 5:16 says, "Rejoice always." The Herrin Family Translation of that verse is: Celebrate always. As followers of Jesus, it is not just a suggestion to celebrate when things are good. It's commanded to celebrate at *all* times. If our celebration is predicated on our moods, bank accounts, social media engagement, or number of friends, we are simply not celebrating correctly.

I'm not saying that celebrating always is easy. It is definitely not. I fail pretty regularly at celebrating in bad times. But it is worth the fight.

I'm reminded of two guys in the Bible named Paul and Silas, who got thrown into prison for something they shouldn't have. They had no idea what was going to happen. There was a chance they would spend a long time in that jail cell. There was even a chance they could be killed. It was the definition of a "bad time," and yet it did not stop their celebration. They began praising God, singing, and celebrating the God they served. Around midnight, their celebration caused an earthquake that shook the foundation of the prison; the doors flew open, and their chains came off. They were free men. One of the guards ended up giving his life to Christ.

This story of Paul and Silas in Acts 16 is really cool. It can be our really cool story, too. Horrible things happen in life. I am not trying to downplay trauma, sadness, loss, or any other heartbreaks. But there is always, no matter the situation, something worth celebrating. Paul and Silas celebrated the goodness of God. They didn't really have much else. They hit rock bottom, but quickly found out that God could be their Rock at the bottom.

Maybe pain or disappointment won't go away immediately, but maybe, like Paul and Silas, we can find God in the middle of it. Maybe our ability to celebrate hardship—when no one else would even think about celebrating—can become a witness to people no one else can reach. What if our celebrating in all things helps all kinds of people come to know Christ?

HABIT: CELEBRATE EVERYTHING

We've talked about celebrating and a few of the ways we can celebrate. Now it's up to us to become walking and talking parties everywhere we go. God wants us to be full of joy. Not as-the-world-gives joy, but as-He-gives joy. Joy found in the beauty and wonder of His creation, in others, and ultimately in Him.

Celebrating everything is about the journey, not the destination. There will always be room for improvement in this habit, so don't beat yourself up if you fall short. Just keep getting back up every day with the intention of celebrating.

My wife has had a reminder on her phone for 4 p.m. that has gone off every single day since I've met her. It says *Have you found the gold today?*

She is further along in her journey of celebrating everything than I am, and can normally delete her reminder quickly because she's been celebrating all day long. But every once in a while, she will see the reminder and call a friend. Or she might look at me and say something kind that she thought earlier in the day but never said out loud.

If you want to take a practical step in developing the habit of celebrating, set your own reminder. Maybe you do it on your phone like Maddy, or maybe you should put a sticky note on your mirror or car door. The how doesn't matter. Just be sure to put yourself in a position to remember that celebrating is worth it.

Another cool thing that has worked for me has been public celebration. A few years ago, I started posting "Gonna be the best day ever" every single day on my Instagram story. It was kind of corny at first, but it quickly became something I couldn't wait to do. It is a small, daily celebration when I reflect and thank the Lord for all of the new opportunities and joy that I get to experience that day. And it began to catch on.

There have been a few times over the years when I have forgotten to post it first thing in the morning, and my inbox will quickly be flooded with people saying things like "Where is the best-day-ever post today?" or "Did you forget something?" There is nothing like the public accountability of Instagram. (Ha!)

Maybe you don't post a celebration every day, but you can look at your own daily rhythms or places you spend a lot of time and find simple ways to make celebrating part of your routine. Remember, the more you intentionally celebrate, the more you will naturally celebrate.

OUTRO

Congratulations! You've read all of *Holy Habits* (or maybe you flipped to the back of the book to read the last page—in that case, go back to the front!). I hope this book has encouraged you in some way in your pursuit of Jesus. That was my hope, prayer, and goal every minute I spent writing it.

Habits were never the goal; Jesus was and is! But I firmly believe our habits are the best vehicles to drive us into a deeper relationship with the Lord.

There is an unbelievable opportunity as the world gets darker for the Church to shine brighter. There is a never-before-seen opportunity for the Church to be a place full of deep people in a world increasingly inching toward the shallows. I'm reminded of Jesus' words in Matthew 5:13–14:

You are the salt of the earth. But if the salt loses its saltiness, how can it be made salty again? It is no longer good for anything, except to be thrown out and trampled underfoot. You are the light of the world. A town built on a hill cannot be hidden.

We cannot impact the world if we look just like the world. When people see us, they must see something different, something deeper. Something attractive. They must see a better way. Ultimately, they must see Jesus living inside of us.

Let's take one more look at the ten holy habits you've read about in this book.

1. Read It and Choose It (obey Scripture)
2. Get Good at Coming Home (repent often)
3. The 1-Minute Prayer (pause to pray in 1-minute increments during the day)
4. Take a Day to Rest (practice sabbath)
5. Keep It Simple (practice contentment)
6. Find a Coach (be discipled)
7. Be a Coach (make disciples)
8. Sit in Silence (make space for God to speak)
9. Contribute to a Team (join a local church)
10. Celebrate Everything (practice gratitude)

It is my prayer for every person reading this book that through your habits, your relationship with Jesus would deepen to new levels of intimacy and cause you to thrive in a world that is desperately looking for hope. That these habits would lead to better marriages, neighborhoods, friendships, businesses, schools, governments, and cities. My prayer is that the people in your circle would look at your life and see not someone perfect, but someone whose joy, peace, and purpose are not diminished when situations change. That they would see someone steadfast, enduring, and firm in who they are. That they would see you and want to know how they can have what you have, and that you would be willing and ready to show them that Jesus is for everyone.

Our world does not need better preachers. We don't need better churches. We need people who are better at day-to-day living. We need people who look different because they are different. We need people who do not just know the Bible but are being transformed by its truth.

Here is my encouraging final message of this book: If your city is going to be changed for Jesus, no one else is coming. Reinforcements are not on the way. Jesus is not coming back until the final day. It's up to us now. The good news is, we don't have to do it alone. Thank God for the Holy Spirit.

Our cities can be changed for Jesus. I believe they *will* be changed for Jesus. Not because we host an amazing conference or because our branding on social media is catchy or clever. But rather, because we are becoming more and more like Christ, one holy habit at a time.

ACKNOWLEDGMENTS

There are so many things I could say and people I could thank for helping make this book possible, but I will try to be brief.

Maddy Herrin—Thank you for teaching me how to follow Jesus. You are my best friend and sacrifice so much for me and our family. The true MVP of our family. There is no way this book would have happened without you. I love you.

Mom and Dad—For showing me that prayer is worth it. The prayers you prayed for your family are still growing a harvest. Thank you for modeling that for me as I have started my own family. I look up to you and love you more than you could possibly know.

Lion—For sleeping in every morning until seven so I could get up early and write this book. I love you, kid!

Karson Herrin—For being the boldest girl in the world. I'm so lucky to have a sister like you. Your faith (and sometimes stubborn faith) has given me so much inspiration over the years, including as I was struggling to write this book.

WayChurch—For letting me be your pastor and for pushing me to take private habits into a public space. It is a dream come true to follow Jesus and reach the city of Nashville with you guys. Thank you.

Richard Foster—Your writing is directly responsible for helping me see Jesus more clearly. I've never read a book outside of the Bible that has impacted me more than your *Celebration of Discipline*. I hope to thank you for it one day in heaven.

Dallas Willard—For helping me see that being an apprentice of Jesus is something that needs to be done thoughtfully and intentionally but that there is also room for spontaneity and beauty. Your writing has blessed me.

Grant Skeldon—For helping me see that discipleship did not have the priority in my life that it should. You have been an incredible gift in my life spiritually and an even greater friend.

Micah Mac—Thanks for sharpening me, bro. Many of the ideas that have come out of our conversations were springboards for material in this book. I love you like a big brother.

My agent, Tom Dean—Thank you for your belief in me over the years and the encouragement to push this idea out of me. You have been a consistent and life-giving friend that I would trust with anything.

My editor, David Sluka—You have been incredible. Thank you for taking a chance on me when you didn't have to. I am unbelievably grateful.

NOTES

Introduction

1. Richard J. Foster, *A Celebration of Discipline: The Path to Spiritual Growth*, 3rd ed. (San Francisco: HarperCollins, 1998), 1.

2. James Clear, *Atomic Habits: An Easy and Proven Way to Build Good Habits and Break Bad Ones* (New York: Avery, 2018), 38.

Habit 1 Read It and Choose It

1. This concept in the context of marriage is also discussed in Gary Thomas's bestseller *Sacred Marriage: What If God Designed Marriage to Make Us Holy More Than to Make Us Happy?* (Grand Rapids: Zondervan, 2018).

Habit 3 Talk to God

1. Leonard Ravenhill, *Why Revival Tarries* (Minneapolis: Bethany House, 2004), 26.

2. E. M. Bounds, *Power through Prayer* (Chicago: Moody, 2009), 40.

3. Ravenhill, *Why Revival Tarries*, 44.

Habit 5 Keep It Simple

1. L. Ceci, "Average time spent daily on a smartphone in the United States 2021," Statista, June 14, 2022, https://www.statista.com/statistics/1224510/time-spent-per-day-on-smartphone-us/.

2. John Piper (@JohnPiper), "One of the great uses of Twitter and Facebook will be to prove at the Last Day that prayerlessness was not from lack of time," Twitter, October 20, 2009, https://twitter.com/JohnPiper/status/5027319857.

3. Foster, *Celebration of Discipline*, 87.

4. Foster, *Celebration of Discipline*, 81.

Habit 6 Find a Coach

1. Grant Skeldon, *The Passion Generation* (Grand Rapids: Zondervan, 2018), 61.

Habit 8 Sit in Silence

1. Foster, *Celebration of Discipline*, 15.

2. N. T. Wright, "3-Mile an Hour God," *Godspeed*, documentary film created by Matt Canlis, 2016, 36:53, https://www.livegodspeed.org/watchgodspeed-cover.

3. Rich Villodas, *The Deeply Formed Life* (Colorado Springs: Waterbook, 2021), 22.

Habit 9 Contribute to a Team

1. Timothy Keller (@timkellernyc), "@JeffersonBethke You are the generation most afraid of real community because it inevitably limits freedom and choice. Get over your fear," Twitter, July 29, 2013, https://twitter.com/timkellernyc/status/361923004965462017?lang=en.

Habit 10 Celebrate Everything

1. Daniel Gilbert, *Stumbling on Happiness* (New York: Alfred A. Knopf, 2006).

Noah Herrin is a pastor and public speaker based in Nashville, Tennessee. Noah graduated from Lee University in 2016 with a bachelor's degree in communications before founding a college ministry called the Gathering. The Gathering movement reached thousands of young adults on a weekly basis and eventually led to Noah traveling around the country to share the life-changing message of the Gospel at churches, universities, and conferences.

In 2022, Noah and his wife, Maddy, and son, Lion, moved to Nashville, Tennessee, to start a new church called Way Church, launching in 2023.

When Noah is not enjoying time with family or speaking/ministering, he enjoys playing golf, competing in board games, reading, playing pickleball, and eating Chick-fil-A. His ideal day would be doing all of those things with friends and family with a forty-five-minute power nap right after lunch followed up by a hot pour-over coffee.